SOLOS

ALSO BY AL BASILE

A Lit House – 100 poems, 1975-2011
Tonesmith – 100 poems, 2012-2016

CDs

Down on Providence Plantation
Shaking the Soul Tree
Red Breath
Blue Ink
Groovin' in the Mood Room
The Tinge
Soul Blue 7
At Home Next Door
The Goods
Woke Up in Memphis
Swing n' Strings
B's Expression
Mid-Century Modern
Quiet Money
me & the Originator
B's Hot House
Last Hand

PLAYS

Flash Blind, an audio verse play featured as a podcast at the HEARnow Festival of audio theater, summer 2020

FICTION

Play of the Game/La Jugada del Partido
(a short story with translation)

SOLOS

One Hundred Poems, 2017-2020

Al Basile

Antrim House
Bloomfield, Connecticut

Copyright © 2021 by Al Basile

Except for short selections reprinted for purposes of
book review, all reproduction rights are reserved.
Requests for permission to replicate should
be addressed to the publisher.

Library of Congress Control Number: 2021930363

ISBN: 978-1-943826-78-0

First Edition, 2021

Printed & bound by Ingram Content Group

Book design by Rennie McQuilkin

Front Cover painting: "There'll Never Be Another Rudy Vallee"
by Robert G. Hamilton, 1995

Author photograph by Meghan Sepe

Antrim House
860.217.0023
AntrimHouseBooks@gmail.com
www.AntrimHouseBooks.com
400 Seabury Dr., #5196, Bloomfield, CT 06002

To those readers who are finding out for the first time that poetry can be an antidote to the poison of our times.

Acknowledgments

My thanks to the editors of the following publications, where these poems first appeared, sometimes in earlier versions.

Literary Imagination: "The Bee's Lot," "The Dead Are Otherwise Engaged"
Five Points: "Blues Primeval"
Literary Matters: "How I Learned About Parenting"

me & the Originator (a poem and song CD: the author's reading of these poems are included as audio tracks on the CD and printed in the accompanying booklet) *Sweetspot Records* 9862, 2018:

"The Trunk"
"What He Carried"
"Useless Good Advice"
"Self-Reliance"
"The Bee's Lot"
"What He Deserved"
"Learn to Draw!"
"Breaking Up is Hard to Do"
"Who Owns It?"
"Solo"
"Young and Old"
"Confessing the Blues"
"How It Goes"

Thanks to David Cashman, Rhina Espaillat, and Christopher Ricks for being my most faithful and sympathetic readers, and to the Powow River Poets for their helpful comments on some of these poems in workshop settings.

The author's reading of the poems included in this book may be accessed at http://www.albasile.com/Solos_-_audio_files.html.

Table of Contents

A Case for Meaning / 3
A Dream Gem, Revisited / 4
A Private Conversation / 5
A Trick of the Light / 9
A Worn Coin / 10
About My Positive Attitude / 11
All Goodbyes Ain't Gone / 12
An Eastern European Mystery / 14
An Onstage Silence / 16
An Ordinary Story / 19
Ancient Roman, 1972 / 21
Another Harmony / 22
Answers From the Magic 8 Ball / 23
As If It Were So / 24
Bad Money Drives Out Good / 26
Bad Rug / 28
Best Wishes, Bill Russell / 29
Bittersweet / 31
Blues Primeval / 32
Building the Artificial Woman / 34
Calluses / 36
Christmas, 2017 / 38
Concerning Trust / 39
Cootie Sets Me Straight / 40
Cut Lines / 43
Danse Légère / 45
Delayed Performance / 46
Dynamite Hill / 47
Early Steps / 49
Eating Cherries / 51
Empty Houses / 52
Falling Asleep / 79
Finishing the Almond Crescent / 80
from *me & the Originator* / 81
   1. The Trunk / 81
   2. What He Carried / 82

    3. Useless Good Advice / 83
    4. Self-Reliance / 84
    5. The Bee's Lot / 85
    6. What He Deserved / 85
    7. Learn to Draw! / 86
    8. Breaking Up is Hard to Do / 87
    9. Who Owns It? / 88
    10. Solo / 90
    11. Young and Old / 91
    12. Confessing the Blues / 91
    13. How It Goes / 92

His Neighbor's Take / 93
Holding My Breath / 95
How I Learned About Attraction / 96
How I Learned About Blindness / 98
How I Learned About Parenting / 99
How I Learned About Supply and Demand / 101
How I Learned About Time / 103
How I Learned to Love Mozart / 105
How It Happens / 108
I Fall While Running / 109
In Service of the Word / 110
In the Fourth Quarter / 117
In the Later Rounds / 118
Joy to the World / 119
Kingdom of Despair / 120
Krazy Kat and Junk on the Moon / 121
Light Breaks In / 122
Living in the Future / 123
Naming Rights / 124
New Year's Eve / 126
No Entry / 127
One Goes to Zero / 128
Only the Dead Are Perfect / 129
Other Waters of March / 130
Paeanster to Punster / 131
Palimpsest / 132
Parra Makes a Point / 134
Playing the Solo / 135
Riders on the Climb / 137

Running Downhill / 138
Solstice Song / 139
Some Words / 140
Something Has Happened / 141
Something Simple But Hard to Do / 142
Speaking Parts / 143
Splitting the Pod / 145
The Art of Time / 146
The Bells of Paradise / 148
The Biblical Span: On Turning Seventy / 151
The Brave / 152
The City Dweller Copes with Quarantine / 153
The Dark Preserve / 154
The Dead Are Otherwise Engaged / 155
The Deadliest Are Not Like You and Me / 156
The Fearless / 157
The Gift / 197
The Magi Lose Their Way / 199
The Next Idea / 201
The Rise of a Sparrow / 202
The Substitute / 203
The Sweetest Sound / 205
The Tree That Didn't Know It Was a Fruit Tree / 206
The Unforgivable / 208
The Uses of Ignorance / 211
Through a Window / 212
To a Young Singer / 214
Too Green / 215
Trickling Up the Jug / 218
Unanswered Prayers / 219
Unofficial Love / 220
Using an Accent / 221
Why Don't You Get Back to Me? / 222
You Have Reached Your Destination / 223
You Want It Simple / 224
Your Feelings, No / 226
Youth in Age / 227

About the Author / 229
About the Book / 230

Author's Note

Each poem in this collection may be considered a transcription of a performance, and like the transcription of a jazz solo, the notation on the page is an important aid to understanding, but not a substitute for, the performance itself. Any or all of the performances here may be heard by following this link: http://www.albasile.com/Solos_-_audio_files.html.

SOLOS

A Case for Meaning

Light was alive before the eye to see it,
granting some worm an edge that urged the organ
into being, the better for the bearer
to survive. Selection over time
bred sight into successful organisms.

Or was the visible also (or only)
finding a way to realize itself
more completely through a vehicle,
emerging into new versions of power?
The eye, in seeing, licenses the light.

By being conscious, we are sensitive
to time, susceptible to consequence:
meaning is made perceptible to us.
The organ of discernment is refined,
the better to prepare us for a world
where someone's reasons lurk behind the curtain.

Meaning is real in us; we are its agents,
the first through whom it can confirm itself.
Both in and of the world, we license it
the better to equip us for the real.
Declare all meaningless at your own peril!
Deny the light, condemn yourself to darkness.

A Dream Gem, Revisited

A rarity, such prescience in a dream:
fast in a long-lost lover's mid-embrace,
to feel the warming fullness of acceptance
as something real, and know it wouldn't last
past waking, but to hold on still, as long
as the protection of the dream affords,
because the warmth will keep in memory.

Like the brick my Nana heated in
the oven, wrapped with care in old newspaper
to lie under the covers by her feet
on bitter winter nights in tenements:
like that, but not for her, who felt the heat
as real; for me instead, for whom it lives
on only as a displaced memory.

A Private Conversation

Out of nothing it came,
out of the forest loam,
out of dark night
where lay the crowns of Nineveh.
                W. B. Yeats

Events of moment, from my student days:
one speaks up, brightly lit in memory.
It was a party at my mentor's house
for celebrated guest Anthony Burgess.

He'd finished his required appearances;
this was a chance to settle and unwind
before other commitments took him elsewhere.
The air was thick with writers circling.

His hair combed forward like an Emperor,
he fielded the petitions of the guests,
who hovered just a little bit too close
and pecked away at him for bits of time.

It was a boisterous affair, but with
the movie of *A Clockwork Orange* fresh
in memory, the talk was not about
the studio's ending, which he didn't like.

Nor was he asked of how he crept into
Shakespeare's head in *Nothing Like the Sun.*
We knew enough to keep away from that.
When my chance came, I turned the talk to music.

I knew he'd written symphonies, but not
that, as he said, he'd helped to pay his way
through school by playing standards
in late night stints at well worn pub pianos.

I mentioned that I played and sang in clubs,
all the old songs. He knew the repertoire.
We eyed the corner with the baby grand
across the crowded living room, untended.

His wife Liana, clearly pleased, Italian,
bubbling with pride, liked the idea:
she urged him, calling him Antonio
endearingly, to go to the piano.

We picked our way through unsuspecting guests.
He settled on the bench, and we discussed
the plan of action. He knew all my keys;
they were the ones he'd always used himself.

We started quietly, his eyes cast down,
exchanging notes on "Isn't It a Pity?"
Slipping into character and story
was all the talk of Heine that we needed.

The voices dropped to murmurs in the room,
became an audience. I told myself
it's not for them, but let them overhear
our gossip in the language of the songs.

His chords, my melody a conversation
about the stories of Berlin and Gershwin,
Porter, Dietz and Schwartz, and Harry Warren,
each of us listening for the other's views.

And it went on for hours, as I remember,
us carrying the music in our arms,
sealed off from writers jockeying for wit.
We had escaped into a private world.

At least that's how I always told the story;
but maybe it was just a song or two.
Once your imagination goes to work
the story can become your memory.

After forty years or so had passed,
I learned my mentor's wife was still alive.
I wondered on a whim if she remembered.
Since no one now is safe from being found,

out of the blue I sent a message to her,
who must by now be well into her eighties.
Did she recall the party where I sang
while Burgess backed me on her baby grand?

Weeks went by. She was somehow alive,
but nothing came. That's that, I thought. It's gone.
She's wandered too far down some darkened hall,
and she's the only witness left who'd know.

All the other principles have passed;
I never knew the names of half the guests.
So maybe after all it didn't happen,
at least not in the way that I recall.

Then out of a blue that proved to be
identical, back came a clear reply:
"That party! There's no way I could forget it.

You both kept going, far into the night."

The past is gone. What can we call our own?
However bright and warm the memory,
we take a deeper draught of satisfaction
when others sit with us around the fire.

A Trick of the Light

To see a bobber move when poorly lit,
I learned you had to look away from it.
While that felt odd, it didn't do to quibble
when hoping not to miss a nibble.

And it was fine to find in latter days
off-center witness worked in other ways:
the flicker of a flame she meant to banish
would briefly flare before she vanished.

But now the trick's no longer so reliable.
Today my eyes (I find it undeniable),
despite my wisdom in the use of sight,
are often fooled in failing light.

A Worn Coin

Admit it. You're a little curious
about this coin, so old and worn it glows
instead of shining. Smooth, it makes you guess
a number for its age, and what it knows

about the outcome of repeated touch.
It doesn't tell you what you should revere,
name its maker, or reveal how much
was minted of its metal, nor the mere

identity of who will honor it.
How to assess its value? Is it made
of something rare? Would those who hunt for it
prize it for itself and not what's faded

from it? New, its maker struck a claim
into its surface: "Ownership of all
contained is here asserted in another's name."
But none remains to answer to a call.

So now the metal speaks in muted tones:
"Take me for what I'm made of, not for what
those others claimed, for I am mine alone;
learn what I am, and value me for that."

About My Positive Attitude

Deep in my years, alone but not unhappy,
knowing I've been blessed, I lie in bed
awake at midnight, sifting through my childhood,
feeling again how strongly I was loved,

how much my parents loved each other, always.
Just as it's supposed to be, it was –
sorry, not dysfunctional at all.
So who am I to speak of suffering?

It's not for me to beat the drum of loss,
or underline inevitable fall –
that's for those who hold to what is gone.
I focus on refreshment and arrival:

new shoots part the ashes of the spent,
new waters fill a hole poked in the ocean.
What vanishes provides an open space;
I celebrate what's born to take its place.

All Goodbyes Ain't Gone

In memoriam Robert Hamilton, American Painter

When he was teaching, he would go to Maine
to paint each summer. As the season ended,
he would keep new work he liked and throw
away the rest, until one afternoon he found

a piece, unsigned but claimed as his, for sale
in a small Portland shop. The man who brought
it in, when found and questioned, readily
admitted it: he'd got it at the dump.

It had been thrown out, after all; he'd done
nothing wrong. He begged a signature,
in fact, to boost the price. That episode
began the yearly end-of-summer bonfires.

The work which didn't measure up was given
over to the flames, a ritual
that purified the efforts of the season.
The artist would return to work refreshed.

One winter afternoon while he was off
at school, his son and I, with time
to kill, nosing about the house the better
to amuse ourselves, dislodged a box

of color slides from off a hallway shelf.
When held up to the light, each one revealed
a painting in the father's recent style.
"He makes reference slides of all his work,"

his son said, looking carefully. "Don't think
I recognize this batch, although he's used
foam core for the last couple of years.
Let's ask him; he'll be back right after class."

On his return, we showed him what we'd found.
He took the slides out from their plastic wells
and scrutinized each one; not a detail
escaped him. Finally he put them back.

"I thought I took care of these," he said
acidly, and brought them, with a can
of lighter fluid, out to the back yard.
He put a match to them and watched them burn.

An Eastern European Mystery

for T. L.

Ah my dear, I think that we will never
meet. It's been four years since we've been writing,
and while we've known enough to make no promises –
we've never even heard each other laugh –

still, beyond the years and distances
imposed on us, we've touched each other's souls
as words can do. And what we have is rare
enough to wish a chance to find out more.

But now you've said you hope I can be patient,
that you can't write, and don't know for how long.
It's three months now, and just a word or two
have made their way across the world to me.

You've even said that messages I've sent
to you since Christmas have been left unopened.
I know exactly what would make me say
I couldn't write, and didn't want to know

the feelings that we always talked about,
and if it's what I think, I can be patient;
there are times I shouldn't be important.
A pure love hopes, but doesn't make demands.

Now you ask me for a list of films,
both black and white and color, from the Thirties
to the Sixties, and I've given you
a dozen names that everyone should see.

They'll help you with your English, and our culture;
I wonder who you plan to see them with.
But as I think of it, I'll add one more:
make sure you see Hitchcock's *Notorious*.

Where Cary Grant convinces Ingrid Bergman
to play up to Claude Rains, then marry him,
and all to spy on his activities –
but not before Grant falls in love with her.

She carries out the plan, and he is distant,
cold to her, and treats her like a whore
while using her to get the information.
He's torn between his duty and desire,

but if he were to tell her how he felt,
she'd lose the will to keep up the charade.
All through the final reel she's being poisoned;
will rescue come in time, or be too late?

It is a story where indifference
is not to be believed; where silent love
must bide its time in pain and from a distance,
and selfishness is barely kept at bay.

An Onstage Silence

The play is set in Spain, 1600

A moment in the middle of a silence:
five characters unmoving on a stage,
their actions driven inward, each one caught
and paralyzed between conflicting gales.

The father, proud and deeply shamed, extends
with the electric gesture of a hand
the sharp command that none may say a word.
His wife and younger daughters dare not move.

But on their faces all can see their love
and pity for the oldest daughter, come
to beg that she be taken back into
the family deserted for a lover.

Blinded by an illness as a child
she hadn't thought that she'd survive, and since
condemned to brood on her escape, was sure
that Death would soon come back for her. She'd been

unlikely to succumb to love, but once
ensnared, she was forever torn between
her unfamiliar hopes to share a future
and expectations of her certain end.

She'd given up her family's protection
and gone to live in sin with her new man,
knowing how her father would be hurt;
poor as he was, he never could forgive

the damage she would do to his good name
and her rejection of him as a parent.
Let some other man provide for her;
her bond with him was gone, broken forever.

Risking it all, she'd walked away uncertain
of the outcome. When that kind of love,
available to everyone but her
it seemed, proved temporary, she was trapped.

So here she was again, back in that tiny
house whose walls she didn't need to touch
to navigate, her mother and two sisters
close by, as she could tell, but saying nothing.

And he was there, she knew, enforcing silence.
She could feel the women reaching out,
but they were not permitted to acknowledge
her. Torn as they were, they had no choice.

As vividly as she remembered them,
she could imagine each of their expressions,
though since she couldn't see her father's face,
she couldn't tell all it was costing him.

But as the scene played out in front of us,
the audience, the faces on the stage
revealed conflicting feelings in succession
as growing silence twisted up the tension.

As her pleas receded into time,
there came a moment when she realized
she wouldn't be accepted. Suddenly,
her last hope banished, her expression fell.

It's at that point when all the conflict drains
out of their faces. Motionless, the actors
settle into parts of a tableaux
which could have been a still in sepia,

or a painting capturing the group,
its somber palette all the tans and browns
and verging into saturated blacks
used by Murillo when he painted beggars.

An Ordinary Story

It's a time-honored, celebrated tale
from my hometown: how long ago a wagon
barreled up with whiskey sought a short
cut across Kenoza Lake late in
a winter milder than its predecessors.

Out over the expanse, the surface groaned,
cracked, and gave way as the hooves punched through,
and soon the horses, wagon, driver, barrels,
slipped down into the frigid depths, all lost,
except for a faint whiskey tinge that lingered
on thereafter, sweetening the water.

With my new skates in hand one winter day,
I politicked to lift the skating ban
my father had imposed on city lakes.
Responsible for parks and recreation,
he'd sent out a man to take a boring.
"Three inches is enough," I said, "I read it
in the almanac." He was unmoved.
"Five inches," was his answer, and my skate
blades went untested for another week.

The man who drove that team became a legend;
his rash choice sniffed a bit like heroism.
My father didn't lend himself to folk tales.
Because they didn't happen, stories of
those boys who broke through three inches of ice
still go untold, and boys like me live on.

It's in the absence of such accidents
my father's rectitude sweetens the world,
streaming from its ordinary depths.

Ancient Roman, 1972

Dressed in the black of my Sicilian aunts,
imperious as eighty-five can be,
she sat in an Eternal City haunt,
warm to the task of educating me.

"I'm purebred Roman. We go back," she said
fiercely, "two thousand years, unbroken line,
my family!" Pride held up her ancient head;
her voice was thin but certain. "In the time

of Emperors!" She sat back, satisfied,
and peered up at me, who looked like a local
but sounded like l'America. She tried
to gauge my worth, my lineage the focal

point. "And you, where were your people from?"
she slyly asked, and turned a practiced eye
to stare up, as I squinted from the sun
full on my face. Awaiting my reply,

she sat, a judge complacent in the shade.
"My father was Bruzzese, near Calderone,
my mother was Siciliane," I said.
She wrinkled up a grin. "Ah, minestrone!"

Another Harmony

for Rhina Espaillat

You could have been my mother's younger sister.
For fate decreed my soul would sound together
with her only sibling's soul – two bells,
both sturdy, cast alike in bronze, whose tones
were close, on different pitches, with the first
struck earlier, the second set in motion
while the other rang out rich and clear,
related such that each fed energy
to keep the other vibrant. I *did* have
this rare a resonance to nourish me
back then – except my mother had a brother.

Answers from the Magic 8 Ball

I don't know what else to do. Should I
really ask a question? *Outlook good.*

OK, about that woman – was I wrong
to trust her? *Concentrate and ask again.*

Did she lie when she said she'd give up
her other guy? *Better not tell you now.*

Look, I'm not blaming him, I understand.
But can she keep her word? *Don't count on it.*

Is that it? Does she mean well, but is just
too weak to make it stick? *Without a doubt.*

So I'm a dope if I don't give her up,
is that what you're saying? *It is certain.*

But what if I'm too weak myself? Suppose
I'm just too hung up? *As I see it, yes.*

Then whatever I decide won't matter,
she'll be leaving. *Outlook not so good.*

So is she going to stay or go? I need
some kind of answer. *My reply is no.*

Should I make up my own mind, or should I
keep asking questions? *My reply is no.*

Are you going to help me out at all?
Situation cloudy – ask again.

As If It Were So

That grades and comments weekend I was not
fit company. She went out to the island
with her childhood friends. I stayed up late
with paperwork and went to bed exhausted.

The phone woke me at 2 AM. Her voice
was distant, frantic, at a pitch of fear
I'd never heard in it before, declaring
I should do something, anything, to help.

It started out as harmless fun; they'd been
amusing themselves with a Ouija board.
A voice had broken through: a boy, confused,
not knowing where he was, missing his mother

and bleeding from a knife wound to the belly,
begging that they not break the connection.
They'd had a laugh, and put the board away.
Susceptible, she found she couldn't sleep.

I told her to get out the board again;
we'd summon him and re-establish contact.
Some who died a violent death, I said,
not knowing they were dead, were not at rest

and wandered, neither here among the living
not there among the dead, lost on the way.
It was silent in the room. I kept
the phone up to my ear and heard more silence

at the other end. Her friends were all

asleep. At last she came back on the line.
Holding the receiver tight between
her shoulder and her cheek, she freed her hands.

The board in place, the planchette at the ready,
she called out to the boy by name. And soon
enough the answers came, and she relayed them
to me, so we could talk to him together.

As though to any other frightened child,
we told him calmly of his situation,
and simply said his mother had gone on
ahead, but in the opposite direction,

away from where our voices seemed to be.
We said that she'd be waiting for him there,
and he must hurry, for she would be worried,
and eager for them to be reunited.

And when he seemed at last to understand,
we asked for him to say goodbye, and then
not to respond if we should ask again,
to show us he had gone. After the letters

spelled it out, we got no further answers.
Her relief was palpable, across the distance
which separated us. Her voice, untroubled,
was once again the one I loved to hear.

The grip of fear, in this world for the next,
felt by the living or the dead, is real.
No matter whether I believe or not,
dissolving it is good enough for me.

Bad Money Drives Out Good

From the ERA of southpaw pitchers
to the highest dudgeon in the roles
of Eric Blore, to know the trivia once
ennobled both the subject and the search.

Now algorithms cut right to the chase,
flipping over all the cards: no effort,
need to memorize, or love the game.
Both enterprise and outcome are devalued.

Answers are cheap and spit out quickly now
across the screens. The questions settle deeper:
which are true, and which meant to mislead?
People lie; assertions look alike.

Not only is reality at stake;
the search itself, reduced to finding out
what's fake, is superficialized.
The greater truth sinks down out of our reach.

Where do we go to learn humility
which honors the emotions of another,
which sees another's needs as equal to
our own – and more, which makes us treat them so?

How to lend value by attention paid
to listening, and being of a mind
to change as a result of what we hear?
How to work, instead of wait, for answers?

As object of a lifelong search, what chance
has wisdom got? There is no guarantee
we'll find it here, where no one even knows
of Lefty Grove and his 300 wins.

Bad Rug

It was obvious, but no one said it;
I suppose he thought we all were fooled.
Small children stared in wonder, wobble-jawed
as perfect thick-close stitching overruled

that broad expanse of scalp, and capped it like
an acorn. Adults, we averted eyes
and focused on his brow, declarative
and sure, oblivious to all that lies

above. And we played ignorant, until
he reached to friends for help at his first slip
and toppled off that high, uncertain perch,
leaving an empty wrapper in their grip.

Best Wishes, Bill Russell

I consider Bill Russell, the center and later player-coach of the Boston Celtics from 1957-69, to be the greatest team player and leader in sports history. His teams won championships in college (2), the Olympics, and the NBA (11). He has more rings than fingers and thumbs; he wears only his first, from 1957, and his last, from 1969. He wrote of teammate Sam Jones that he could have scored thirty a night, but preferred to give the team whatever it needed to win in any situation, an example of what Russell calls "team ego."

Sitting behind a table, pen in hand,
goatee, mustache, and sideburns curly white,
he read the words I'd written on a card.
Some thirty years before, he'd never sign

at all; instead, he'd shake your hand. But now
a book tour brought us face to face. Two hundred
of us were given cards on which to write
the sentiment we hoped he would inscribe.

Mine said "To Sweet Al, the Sam Jones of trumpet
players." Russell didn't lift his head,
but peering at the card he simply said
"Well, I can't write this," in a neutral voice.

"I know," I said, "you've never heard me play.
But I just wanted to get your attention.
And I really want to see the rings –
is it true you wear the first and last?"

Now he looked up. His eyes were bright and crinkling.
There was the grin I'd seen a hundred times
light up his face after another win.
He made two fists and put his hands together.

The first one was from Nineteen Fifty Seven;
chiseled into gold, the numerals
were wrapped around a shamrock, and the stone
was modest. On the other hand, the second

was heftier, its diamond centered, deep
embedded in a ball against an emerald
background, rounded by *World Champions*,
and *Boston Celtics, 1969*.

"Thanks," I said, "and may I shake your hand?"
He offered, and my hand was gobbled up.
Smiling, he took my book, reached for his pen
and wrote out his left handed sentiment.

Not until I got outside the building
did I look to see. He'd put a flourish
on the first *T* and the final *l*.
It read *To Sweet Al, best wishes, Bill Russell*.

Bittersweet

Over the last few years the bittersweet
has choked the hedge around my property.
The wrought iron feeder that I drove into
the ground nearby is likewise overrun.

Unstoppable, the twisting tendrils curl
around the metal troughs and keep the birds
from lighting there to feed, so I no longer
see or hear them from my kitchen window.

I'll never stop the bittersweet; it will
outlast me. But if I can cut and clear away
the vines enough to let the iron stand free,
for now and for a little while to come

the jays and cardinals will dart down again
from far beyond my yard, and peck the seeds
I leave, and not the berries on the vines,
so colorful and seeming-innocent.

Blues Primeval

New Year's Eve, 2017

His mother threw him out when he was ten.
She sold her own hand-written gospel songs
for pennies on the street, would not abide
his wanting to sing blues, the devil's music.

"Ain't no love like your mother's love," he'd say
later in life, "I missed a lot." Just days
before he died, he asked his wife to call
long distance to his mother. If he ever
needed her, he said, the time was now.
His mother heard her only son's request.
She put down the phone and walked away.

A year before that end, we opened for
Wolf and his band in Burlington, Vermont.
His kidneys had been damaged in a crash,
and he had shrunk down sixty pounds or so
from the three hundred that he'd bragged about.
The every-other-day dialysis
at VA hospitals along his tour
routes got him through to every other night.

He'd only do six songs, but he still crawled
on hands and knees, and lolled the mike
between his legs, and cooed and howled, ever
the Wolf, an elemental force of nature.

I saw him sitting by himself backstage

after his set, and felt the need to talk.
At rest for now, he was approachable,
burned down body banked back to a stillness,
voice thinned to a thread, unthreatening.

I asked him about Aberdeen, where he'd
been born, and did he ever go back there?
"That's my home," he said, as though that was
an answer. "Well, with all you have to go
through every day to keep this up," I said,
"you must love to play." His great gray head
turned toward me then. Lizards of flame flashed up
into his eyes, his face. 'I'LL DIE ON STAGE!"

Building the Artificial Woman

The first attempts were beautiful but perfect.
So flaws were added, which was an improvement.
A voice came next, to make sounds of approval,
and customers began to ask for movement.

That was enough to satisfy the many,
but some began to clamor for expression,
at least to mimic registering pleasure.
A discerning few made a confession:

They hankered after giving it free will.
Being chosen wasn't any fun
when all the votes were counted in advance
and all the choices narrowed down to one.

They wanted something personal – to feel
loved, when love might well have been withheld
by one who offered company each day
and chose to stay without being compelled.

This proved a challenge, but the next design
was a best seller. Then there came a man
who took exception to the operation.
"I want," he said, "what isn't in your plan.

I want someone to disagree, but stay;
who tells me when I'm wrong, and makes me see
how to do better, but still leaves the chance
to me to make the same mistake again.

Who likes to pay attention to attention,
but understands it when I sometimes don't.
When she's invited to take sides against me,
she'listens diplomatically, but won't.

Who asks me if I like it first, but wears
a hat because she likes to wear a hat,
and when I compliment her on her choice,
she doesn't worry what I mean by that.

Who thinks my chicken cutlets are sublime.
and moves the car when I'm too beat to drive.
Who laughs because she gets I'm being funny,
and smiles because it's hard to be alive.

Who'll never be a servant or a master
but wants to work together as a team,
and build over a lifetime love familiar,
instead of holding out for love supreme.

Can you put all that into a machine?"
The builders smiled. "If that's the way you feel,
what you want is a woman. What we make
are fakes. But most prefer them to the real."

Calluses

1.

Fingertips press firm against the strings
which yield down to the fret and board, then bite
back into the soft flesh of the beginner.
Dull pain's the price of keeping up the fight

between the fingertips, which feel so much,
and drawn out steel which will not be compressed.
Gripping harder, bending strings result
in red and rawness, subtle nerves distressed

and voicing their complaint. By then the goal's
to build up calluses to silence pain.
Through constant use and studied disregard
of everyday discomfort, loss and gain

make their exchange, and thicker skin
allows the hand its liberties against
the board in pain-free comfort. As for what
the newly deadened fingertips can sense,

there's little to report. To drum them on
a tabletop is easier heard than felt.
But put the instrument back in its case
and go on with your life. Calluses melt,

the flesh softens again, and you can feel
to guide the button to the buttonhole.
This happens by itself, without your effort;
your body knows renewal is its goal.

2.

I cried at every slight, real or imagined,
as a baby. Over time I learned
to toughen up. Nobody wants to hear
about it every single time you're burned.

Disappointment, too, is better handled
by an even temperament. Why make
a face at everyone who lets you down?
They mostly think of you for their own sake.

Patience, the virtue: always good to have.
You learn how not to get too soon excited
about an outcome which will take its time.
Love too soon pressed is too soon unrequited.

Long practiced in the ways of self-protection,
well armored now against pangs of the heart,
I ask myself what joy can penetrate
beneath my even temperament, and start

to soften back the mechanism to
its tender state. What must I disavow,
what daily repetition discontinue?
A reawakening awaits me now,

but how to get down to the feeling part,
so buried under layers of control
applied against the tissue of the heart –
how to repay the price of being whole?

Christmas, 2017

These early winter days I rise in darkness,
 rely on bathroom light to guide me out
of sleep, up to the point where I can take
a blade across my face and leave it whole.

Today there is no light. A kitchen fuse,
blown and replaced since yesterday, somehow
has axed the bathroom by association.
The switch is felt for, flipped, and mocks the hand.

The basement fusebox bears a partial key,
hand written, pencilled in over the years,
but there are gaps; there is no "upstairs bathroom."
Replacing those unlabelled doesn't help.

The role of central government has failed;
eventually I give up and go local,
a place-it-anywhere LED dome
affirms the case for independent light.

Still all is not as it was meant to be.
And knowing how it drains the batteries,
I choose to light the room judiciously,
and often opt to labor on in darkness.

Concerning Trust

So easily lost, and so slow to regain:
one small betrayal, and it disappears.
Apparently to be sorry, and explain,
is not enough. But, still remaining, there's

the simple truth, that he who's been left lonely
has misunderstood, and often heatedly
denied, that trust is built in one way only:
promises made, and kept, repeatedly.

Cootie Sets Me Straight

Duke Ellington Concert, Providence College 1968

He was one of my heroes;
most of them were dead,
but here he was, still playing,
and back again with Duke,
where'd he'd first made his name.
In his sixties now,
he'd distilled his sound,
and his intensity
made every note he played
a crack in the night sky.

He was on a break,
sitting motionless,
as though to summon up
the energy he'd need
to get through the next set.
He'd played majestically,
fiercely, vehemently.
His plunger made him vocal.
He spoke in Bubber Miley's
language, but he'd made
it dangerous, more violent.

I went up soberly
and complimented him,
and tried to show I wasn't
just another fan.
I was a player, in

a style designed to be
much like his own. I loved
the players that he loved,
and learned from them as well.
I tried not to sound dumb.

I said, "I play plunger
too, but all I have
is the red-walled kind,
and when you pinch and choke
it off, it sounds too thin.
The one you use has black
rubber walls; it's stiffer
and it's thicker, so
it gives a better sound.
Where can I go to find
a plunger just like yours?"

He looked at me. His head
was massive, powerful;
his cheeks would bulge, he played
so hard. I knew myself
the pressure shook you down
to your spine every time,
and afterward it felt
like you'd gone ten rounds
with a body puncher.

He paused a while, as though
to think of a response;
or maybe it was more
deciding he would answer.
He seemed very tired.

He raised his chin an inch,
and looked straight down at me.
His eyes were glowing white,
deep-set in anthracite.
He said, "You go to
a hardware store – you'll *find*
what you're looking for."

I said, "I don't mean
this wrong, but every town
we go to, I look in
a hardware store, and I
just can't seem to find
a plunger with that nice,
thick black rubber like
the one you use, that gives
a deep, dark sound like that."

He cocked his head a bit
and let out a breath.
He looked down at me,
and he said "You go to
a hardware store – you'll *FIND*
what you're looking for!"
I could see his point,
so I left him alone.

Cut Lines

Your friend told me today you have dementia,
and wouldn't recognize me if I called.
Your intelligence had been a blade
without a handle, honed to such an edge
it drew your blood whichever way you grasped it.

Slicing the real with sensitivities
which complicated everything they cut,
you were forever finding extra meaning
in the signals all around you, feeling
every one was sent to you alone.

You saw your life, ill-starred, as magnified,
and half believed you brought on the disasters
which dogged your days yourself; the other half
was earnest searching in the ordinary
for sunlit places you could stand with others

not Fate-complicit, so their lives just happened.
The outcome of your struggle wasn't clear
when I had loved you though I had the sense
that right or wrong, the faith I had to have
in you could never figure in the balance.

How now to think of you, the question moved
beyond both answers, your intensity
either gone mercifully dull, or set
on endless, multiplying lacerations,
no way for me to know, or you to tell?

And what to say about the memories
we shared, the filaments our souls cast out
to fix upon each other, those that bound us
in the secret ways no one could cut,
rooted in me still, loose ends adrift?

Danse Légère

Brown University, November 1966

Lying in the narrow single bed
with the opera singer's gorgeous daughter,
faces close and bodies touching, pairs
of headphones bringing us the disembodied
thrill of voices nestled in the plush
orchestral fabric of the BSO,
Charles Munch directing us unerringly
through *Daphnis and Chloe*, I was still
but swayed, eyes open, in the dual dance.

The scent of perfume in the harmony
was overpowering, the presence of
the girl as palpable and dense as petals
blown in profusion from the cherry trees,
swirling, drifting deep in layers over me.

When later I returned from dropping
her off back at her freshman dorm, my roommate,
who'd cleared out for the date without a fuss,
revealed he'd hid an open reel recorder
under my bed. Pleased with his enterprise,
he dragged it out, only to find a snarl
of tape it would be hopeless to untangle.
Combined, her weight and mine had bent the springs
enough to jam the moving mechanism.

In vain I tried to tell him: if he could
have listened to the evening unobstructed,
nothing would have been revealed about
the girl and me, our secret, or Ravel.

Delayed Performance

Winter's silence rules; despite delays
which can't enforce its reticence for long,
the sun's advancing incubates the days
and urges all to bursting into song.

So buds, at first present in pizzicato,
tinting melody, then swell throughout
to blossoms' variations in legato.
But for the moment, as though still in doubt

that, full as Nature's impulse has become,
and as it is imperative, tomorrow
it must crescendo from the faintest hum
to roaring color, tones of joy and sorrow

mixed, as they are, might trouble orchestration,
the rest is held, extending hesitation.

Dynamite Hill

That morning I went to the hill alone.
I had green mittens, a black woolen muffler,
and the hat my Mother knit for me,
gray with a red yarn ball on the top.

I'd waxed up the runners on my sled,
a Flexible Flyer, and gone out early,
before the big kids in the neighborhood
got there, to risk a straight shot down the hill.

Other hills around were easier;
my friends and I would always go on them.
This one was steeper, and the runs were sudden;
only big kids went on Dynamite.

My boots crunched on the surface of the snow.
We'd had a thaw, and overnight, a freeze;
the icy hill would be a sheet of glass.
There'd be little I could do to steer.

But then it would be over that much quicker.
I reached the top, then turned, and looking down
I saw the sled tracks, worn between two trees,
glinting sharply in the morning light.

The challenge was to keep between the trees;
hit one and end up in the hospital.
I didn't want to think. I threw the sled
ahead of me and belly-flopped down on it.

Flashing, runners shuddering at once,
I saw I was already headed for
the left tree, and getting to it fast.
I jerked the steering slat with my whole body,

and angled off the worn part of the hill
onto the untracked surface. Gaining speed,
I just had time to see a hidden bump
beyond the tree, and know that I would hit it.

And I was flying; then I hit the road
that went across the bottom of the hill
flush on my belly as if I'd been dropped.
I had the wind knocked out of me, but I

held on until the sled came to a stop,
far into where the rushes used to be,
by the ice edge of the frozen pond.
Way farther than the sledders ever got.

My head cleared, and I got to my feet.
I hadn't wanted anyone to see
me try the hill, and there was no one there.
I had my wish. But now, I had my story.

Early Steps

He had a record player in his bedroom
by the side wall, on a stubby table,
and a row of LPs sitting on the floor.
He'd cribbed a lot of them from the collection
his Dad kept in the living room downstairs.

His Dad loved Bix and Louis, had a special
fondness he reserved for Pee Wee Russell
and all the Condon gang, but he liked modern
too, and featured Rollins and the boppers.
His son had all he needed to get started.

When I'd first met him he was playing harp,
at fifteen, with his own local blues band,
but two years later he had switched to tenor.
He was learning on his own. I didn't know
how far he'd gotten, but one afternoon

I stopped by the house and heard the sax,
so I went up the stairs and down the hall.
When he was practicing, he didn't mind
the company sometimes; he'd just keep playing.
He said "Check this out," and I sat down.

He got the table turning, dropped the stylus
down on the first cut, and settled back,
horn at the ready. Swishing ushered in
two bars of piano introduction.
I knew it was Nat Cole with Lester Young,

the tune "Back to the Land," a blues in F.
Prez had three choruses to start it off.
But just when he came in, the room got bigger:
the tenor on the record came to life,
as it had once in nineteen forty six.

It wasn't just the notes. It was the sound,
the ease, the phrasing, bends, false fingering.
Distinctive separate tones, so closely layered
they blended into something else again –
two kids on one sled, sliding down together.

Or like ghosting footsteps in the snow
to go where someone else has been before,
careful to step in every track the same,
to get the feel of it, before you set
off to make your own, and find your way.

Eating Cherries

This caution, rising from the knowledge that
my teeth are old, and might crack at the shock
of biting down too carelessly, when there
is certainly a pit within the fruit,
is for the moment keeping me from tasting
any sweetness, till I spit it out.

Empty Houses

1

He saw her through the amber diamond panes
as she walked past the old tobacconist's,
and left the shop without a word. He knew
she couldn't be that woman from so long
ago – this one was far too young, as old
as she had been that summer – but he walked
two blocks behind her, bathed in present sunlight
and the uncanny presence of his past.
When passing cars had gotten far enough
ahead, he heard her heels click on the sidewalk.

Then he stopped and let the click fade off;
this was less an encounter, more a call –
but one he wouldn't follow. He undid
his steps back to the shop, apologized
to his old friend for the abrupt departure.
And that was to be all, until the dreams
came, linking the night to nights that followed,
all chapters in an endless river crossing
toward a dim shore, under a bright moon.

The underpinnings of his marriage came
undone then. In his waking hours his wife
and children brought the semblance of no act
before his eyes; he felt himself both actor
and observer, distancing himself.
When after that so much of what he felt
seemed not of his volition, to decide
to leave seemed clear, to do it easier.

2

In another city, where the fall
settles in deliberately, after
careful preparation, but with some
second thoughts on the odd afternoon,
he stood before a half-dismantled house
at windless noon. The demolition men
were off at lunch, heavy equipment idle.
The side wall was down, roof bitten through.
By evening pipework, boards, and dry wall would
have dropped into a heap in the foundation.
But now it gave a doll house look into
the rooms where people had lived out their days.
A host of them had come and gone. He looked
at three rooms on the second floor, and placed
them back into one summer from the past.
Less like his daughter's playhouse then, more like
a theater set, with scenes intensely lit
now in his memory. It happened here,
he realized, but I won't find the answers
here – I've come too late. Still he scoured through
the wreckage later in the afternoon,
and, dogged, came back one more time at night,
armed with a heavy flashlight. When he saw
a face-down snapshot underneath a heap
of lath and plaster, he could feel at once
it was the future reaching out to touch him.
He stepped out carefully across the beams,
collapsed in tangled piles like pick-up sticks,
reached down into the dust, and brought it up.
He scrutinized his prize; drew in his breath.
The light revealed three women sitting on

a gray stone wall, green landscape at their backs,
but it was she – an older she, with traces
of some deep care endured worn on that face,
but unmistakeable. On holiday,
it seemed; no way to know how recently.
.But here were faces to enquire about.

3

Next day he was out early. To the left
of the demolished building, only three
inches of an open door were offered
him, and when he showed the photo through it,
he got no answer for his effort, just
a no, a closing, and the dead bolts turning.

On the other side he had more luck.
A plate below the doorbell said *Boghossian*,
and as he reached to push it he could hear
what sounded like the rushing of deep waters
from beyond, out of the house's depths –
pulsing, ceaseless, somehow cyclical.
Then the door was opened, and the sound
leapt out, articulated into beats,
its rise and fall expressed in swishing patterns.
The man he noticed next was at the door,
stooped a bit, as though he had expected
the intrusion, and accepted it.
Shiny with sweat, his forehead wrinkled up,
then smoothed out where his hairline had receded.
There was sadness in his face when he looked at
the photo; with a hint of resignation

he admitted that he knew the women.
The middle one had died some years before;
the small one on the left, who looked as though
she ate nothing but salads, had moved out
to the other side of town. The last in line,
of course the one that he'd be looking for,
had gone away and hadn't told him where.

The rushing sound stopped suddenly. They went
into a living room, for there was clearly
more to say. The quiet man kept looking
at the photo as a silence filled
the room, and seemed to indicate the time
had come for telling secrets. A dark mole
sat motionless upon his cheek until
he finally spoke, a distance in his voice.

She had moved next door some years ago
and for a while he hardly could believe
his luck. It hadn't stayed that way for long,
though – he knew it was too good to last.

Appearing in a hallway, razor-thin
in black T shirt and jeans, a Zappa-looking
youth stepped in the room and changed the mood.
"I can't find my medium thin crash,"
he said matter-of-factly, and withdrew.

Boghossian stirred as though out of a trance,
went over to a hutch, opened a drawer,
wrote on a piece of paper, and returned.
"The woman on the left, here's her address,"
he said, "and if you find the other one,

give her this, and say that she forgot it."
He offered up a small book bound in leather,
fastened with a golden clasp. "It wasn't
locked," he said, "so what's the difference?
Maybe now I can stop reading it."

The lost look on Boghossian's face stayed with him
like a bitter aftertaste beyond
the closing door, and as he turned away
the distant pounding started up again.
The house pulsed with the swirling rush of cymbals.

4

In the cab that carried him across
the sprawling city to the salad eater,
he dozed and dreamed again about the river.
This time he could see the other shore,
with goats and olive trees in plenty. But
as he kept approaching, it appeared
that longed-for destination kept receding.

The house was set back high above the street.
He climbed a whitewashed set of steps to reach
the door, whose metalwork and frosted windows
let in some light but held back on its secrets.
It opened as he reached the landing, just
as though he'd been expected, and before
he could get out a word, a voice jumped out.
"Look, you tell Harold he should come himself.
He got something that he wants to say to me,

he oughta be a man and come himself."
He was a small man, narrow, maybe thirty,
trying hard to look older and bigger,
in dress pants and suspenders, with a white
V neck T shirt, combed and wetted hair,
bare feet, and a flair for confrontation.
"I can't help it that he doesn't know
the only way to keep Gloria happy.
He should've figured that out first, before
he married her," he went on without stopping,
"But that's not my problem. *I* know how
to keep her happy," he exclaimed, and shifted
so his chest swelled up and jutted out
as though he were a strutting pigeon, paused.

He tried to say that Harold hadn't sent him,
and that he only wanted information,
but there was to be no listening.
"At least I have the decency to park
way down the street. It's more than he deserves,
you know. I'm exercising some discretion,
but that's for her – it's not because of him.
You go back and tell him what I said."

Just then there was a whistle from inside
the house, and the assault of words stopped short.
The little man responded to the summons,
dwindled to a crouch, and scuttled off.
The sun poured partway in behind the door
and lit up a rectangle on the hardwood.

Quiet, chastened now, the man returned,
only a messenger, suddenly smaller.

He listened carefully to the request
about the woman on the right, and took
the photo dutifully. He padded over
the shining wooden floor on his bare feet
and disappeared within. On a side wall
above a sectional, a big Matisse
of nymphs at play shed color in the room.

Returning quickly, still subdued, the man
in the suspenders dipped his glistening head
and handed back the photo, indicating
some writing had been added on its back.
It was a surprise he murmured then –
"Good luck," as though the two of them were friends:
one who'd reached a place from which he wasn't
free to travel; one who could enjoy
the question in the time before the answer.
A softness in his eyes made him look bigger.

5

In a northern city, where the edge
of autumn had already made its mark,
after thirty hours without sleep
which now that he was here he must not give
way to, he shifted sideways on the slatted
wooden bench, not looking at the park
it faced, the children on the swings and slides,
the mothers nearby, talking to each other,
ready to be anxious – he, already
too excited, looked across the street
at the house, its empty driveway showing

him that he'd arrived too late. He would
wait, keep faithful watch, and surely be
rewarded. Her eventual return
would bring an end to this at last; his questions
would be answered. He imagined what
she'd see; it had been years, and he was changed
by marriage, children. Though he couldn't see
how, *she* would – he hoped she'd recognize him.
He in turn would see she was the same.

He pinched his earlobe till it hurt; he mustn't
miss the moment. Just across the narrow
street, the house was waiting too, the first
floor window boxes overflowing with
asters and mums in red and purple, black-
eyed susans bright against the walnut stain
of weathered shingles. He remembered that
she used to have nasturtiums in hanging
baskets in her old apartment – liked
to add their petals to a salad. Color.
She was all for adding color to her life.

He took the small brown book out of his pocket.
It made him feel that he could hear her speak.
He'd looked for his own name in vain; of course,
this was written much more recently.
It wasn't names so much as feelings that she wrote
about. And as he read, he realized
he'd never heard her speak this way, because
with him those feelings had been different.
The quiet man inside the deafening house
had loved too much, his love was suffocating;
although it went unspoken, expectation

weighed her down; his gentleness reproached
her every moment for indifference.
It maddened her that he was understanding.
To move away was all that she could do.

He thought then of the last time he'd been with her.
She had loved too much and he too little;
for different reasons neither would give up.
But on that night her voice was cool and level.
She'd missed her period, she said, and waited.
It felt like a test, and he was young:
he replied by asking the wrong question.
From the way she acted after that,
it was clear that everything was over.
Her last words dried him like a dessicant;
the sound of her voice at the very end
was all that he could take as consolation.

He flushed with shame to think about it now.
Had he come here looking for forgiveness?
Did he even deserve to be forgiven?
Sometimes we don't deserve what we are given,
though, and yet it comes; and he was here.

He'd proved that he could make such a commitment
in the years that followed: to his wife,
his kids, the job; he'd always put them first.
And he'd been tied, but to a stake, not to a mast;
he'd braved no passage, only stood his ground,
been bound by ropes he didn't chafe against.
At last he felt that he could dare the journey –
but would she find him worthy of the test?

A new Volkswagen bug the yellow of
pale daffodils turned up into the driveway,
and she got out, her hair down at her shoulders
in a lazy flip like he had never seen.
He wanted to call out but didn't know
the words, and so he sat straight on the bench
until she'd disappeared behind her door.

In the few minutes that he let go by
he started, stopped, and started once again,
imagining what he would say to her
when she came to the door after his knock.
What would her first expression be, and how
should he begin? Should he speak first, or wait
to see how she reacted, then determine
how best to plead his case? Yes, he would wait.
He got up then and walked across the street.

6

This will be the most unusual
entry in this journal. Circumstances
make it the first in months; that I can make
an entry now seems hardly possible,
and what I have to say is so unlike
what fills the other pages in this book
I might well be thought a different person.

How to explain a knocking at my door
that led me when I opened it into
the most confusing moments of my life?

*How to excuse my acting in a fit
of pique so unlike me I am ashamed?
How, finally, to extricate myself
from the trap in which my weakness caught me?*

*Let me try. I'd just come back from work
yesterday, and hardly had the time
to get changed and begin to decompress,
when I heard a knocking, clear and quiet,
at my door. I opened it to find
a man about my height and size, around
my age, a strange conspiratorial
expression on his face, as though I knew
perfectly well what he was going to say.
He lacked the clipboard of a canvasser,
and anyway he stood there in a green
tweed jacket and a denim shirt, as though
he'd reached some sort of final destination;
he looked about to say "Well, here I am."*

*I was completely sure I didn't know him.
"Yes?" I said. My question said as much,
but keeping his familiar look, he said
"I have an answer to your question now."*

*"I'm sorry," I replied, "I didn't have
a question. Is there something that you want?"
I was sincere; I didn't feel a threat,
and he was clearly after something. Best
to find out what it was.*

                          *He fell back then
a little, turned his head, and spoke again.*

"I understand why you would act as though
we've never met. I do. You chose to break it off
and never deal with me again, I get that.
I don't deserve to be here, really. I accept
that too. But even after all this time, I felt
I had to come — to see how much has changed,
and in what ways. I know you must have changed,
and I can show you that I have as well."

His manner was so certain that his words
forced me to pause; I'm sure I made a face.
"I'm sorry, but you must have me confused
with someone else," I managed to respond.

His look remained untroubled. "As I said,"
he went on, his voice a little lower,
"I see why you feel you have to say
that. But when I say I understand,
I really mean it. Don't you think I know
how much I let you down? I wouldn't blame
you if you never spoke to me again.
But I had to say I'm sorry to your face."

He reached into the pocket of his jacket,
said "Oh yes, here," and handed me this book,
my own, which I had long thought lost, in which
I'm writing now. Something so personal,
and from an unknown hand, jarred me deep down;
this shouldn't be. He shouldn't be, yet here
he was, apologizing for a past
we'd never shared. I took the book and stepped
back from the door. "Come in — let's talk this out,"

I said, and he walked in as though the gates
of heaven had been opened up to him.

"Please, sit," I said, and he sat on the couch.
I took the kendall chair across from him.
"Thank you for this," I said, "I thought I'd lost it.
It's good to have it back. But who you think
I am, and what you think you've done to me,
it's just not so. I don't know who you are,
but I'm very sure we've never met."

He dropped his head a bit, then looked up at me.
"I know I hurt you deeply all those years
ago. It may be easier for you
refusing to admit you ever knew me.
You likely thought we'd never meet again,
and here I show up unannounced. It has
to be a shock. But please, can't we at least
be honest with each other? How can I
speak about the past and what we had
if you won't admit it ever happened?"

The thought got in my head (I don't know why),
that since I wasn't getting anywhere
by telling him the truth he didn't want
to hear, then why not tell the lie he did?
So I got evil for a moment, said
suddenly "All right, have it your way —
you're right. I didn't ever want to see you.
And you know what? I still don't. I can't
forgive you, and I'd rather that you go
away again. Now are you satisfied?"

*I shocked myself with my own words, which struck
him like a ton. He slumped and reeled back then,
the fight gone out of him. He'd given me
so much power over him, and I
had turned it on him just because I could.
It was my turn now to be ashamed.
He lay back on the couch, stunned into silence.
There was no doubt he finally believed me,
but the price I paid to be believed
was high — I'd entered his reality
as someone else whom I could never be,
and never could pretend to be for long.*

*I must confess, the sight of him destroyed
by my rejection, coupled with remorse
over my cruelty, led me to pretend,
for a time, to join him in his world.
Soon enough I'll find out just how long
this spell can last. As I write this today
he's lying in the bedroom, still asleep.*

7

When she opened the door he was prepared
for recognition, quickly followed by
reproach perhaps, or maybe disappointment.
He expected to be put on trial
immediately, their past held against him.
With his first look he saw the lines of care
their time apart had worn into her face
were not so deep as they'd been in the photo.

She had been smiling there with friends, her lips
turned up, her cheeks and eyes in a salute.
But here she was, with hardly an expression,
and right away she stayed behind a mask,
as though he'd been expected, and she'd planned
exactly how she'd play the meeting: feign
ignorance and give him no foothold,
deny that she had anything to do
with him before this moment. Still his voice,
and give the words he told her no good place
to settle. He had not anticipated
seeing him again would make her so
unwilling to acknowledge what they'd shared.
He must have hurt her more than she had showed.
While deepening his shame, it made him more
determined to explain himself. He handed
her the book; the face she made at last
showed recognition, and it seemed she dropped
her guard. And not long after that she broke
down and admitted it, what she'd been doing.
The truth at last. It put them on an equal
footing, let them be themselves to talk,
but her denunciation was so pained
he was struck dumb by his misuse of power.
She'd carried his unworthiness within
for all this time, and he had let it happen.
He never knew he meant so much to her.
To know it made him inconsolable;
and yet she chose this moment to console him.

8

Midway through that first night he knew:
she couldn't be who he was looking for.
She had no anchor scar across her belly.
The doctors cut her open after birth
two ways, and found her insides all mixed up;
they put the pieces in their proper places,
but nobody expected her to live.
And after that there was a recklessness
to what she did that made her fascinating,
if often scary that she lived so hard.

He lay awake and felt her even breathing,
its quiet rise and fall against his chest,
so familiar and yet alien.
This woman hadn't lived that woman's life,
so why had she behaved as though she did?
And how could what she gave him make it seem
he was at last forgiven, just as if
she'd been empowered to act as someone else?

Why had he let her do it? He would ask
himself that many times in years to come;
he never had an answer good enough.
She was, and wasn't, who he'd always wanted:
wrong in fact but somehow rightly true.
And though he felt forgiven, still he knew
that first woman had yet to choose forgiveness,
yet to see how far he'd come from acting
like a selfish child. This cheerful woman,
easy with intimacy, never could:

for she was here, but never had been there.
Yet what she brought to here and now was nothing
less than everything that satisfied
him, short of the answer that he craved.
And so, content for now to have it happen,
he let the moment carry him downstream.

9

When he awoke she had already risen;
he heard her moving in another room.
A line of sunlight through Venetian blinds
had drawn its way up level with his eyelids,
and as he winced and turned his head, the dream
he'd had diffused and slipped back into darkness,
leaving a pang as though he'd dropped his keys
and, helpless, watched them fall into a well.

After he had roused himself and joined her
in the kitchen, talking carefully
while breakfasting on coffee, scrambled eggs,
jam and English muffins, he kept quiet
about his questions; she kept up the game.

He noticed that she didn't talk about
the past, the better to avoid the chance
of being caught in some mistake. She didn't
talk about the future either, since
it was unlikely he'd be fooled for long.

She was tending to some marmalade;
he was pushing eggs around the plate.

The morning light was slanting in the room.
Both were more at ease when they weren't talking.
There was a pile of bills stacked on the table.
His eyes were drawn to the name and address.

"How long have you been using this last name?"

She seemed to catch herself, and finally said,
"I was married for a while, and kept it."
He put the envelope back on the pile.
She picked up the coffee pot from off the stove.
"Want some more?" she asked, and brought it to
the table.

"Sure," he said, "just half a cup."

She poured. "It didn't last too long," she said,
"I mean the marriage. Just two years, no kids."

He sipped it quietly. "Ever been pregnant?"

"No," she said. "There was a scare or two.
Why do you ask? It's kind of personal."

He looked up; he imagined he looked sad.
"Why did you pretend?" he said, "I know.
You're not her. Why make believe you are?"

She dropped her eyebrows for a bit, and then
relaxed, the subtle wrinkles at the corners
of her mouth drew halfway to a smile.

"Oh honey," she said softly, and inclined

her head, "it's just you needed me to be."

He took a last sip, pushed the plate away
and without lifting up his head, said "Now
I have to go. I can't stay here. I have to
go on. To find her, though I know it's crazy,
because I feel like I already found her.
But no. You understand – I have to go."

"Yes," she said, "I know. I'll take your plate."

10

He stood at the reception desk and waited.
Starting back at the beginning hadn't
turned out to be that difficult. The door
that wouldn't open to him when he'd been
there before had opened to him now;
a different sister had come to the door;
her recall went back far enough, and she
had known her neighbors and kept up with them
throughout all the years after they'd moved.
He'd found the address easily enough,
not far away, and still in the same city.
He couldn't quite define the place; it was
too personal to be a hospital.

A summons from the desk brought out a short,
muscular, and cheerful fellow who
could pass for a masseur, or a gym teacher.
He warmed to the assignment right away.
"Happy to help," he said, "she hasn't had

that many visitors the last few years.
I guess you could say that she drives them off."
She always was afraid she'd end this way.
She had mental problems in her family
going back at least three generations.

He led them to an elevator by
the entranceway, and hit the button for the second
floor. The elevator light came on,
and once inside he leaned in to explain.

"Don't get me wrong, she's fine most of the time.
She has her lucid moments. Don't expect
her to know you, though – she'll likely call
you by another name. She gets abusive
sometimes too – there's things she won't forgive
that she keeps blaming everybody for."

The heavy doors slid open. They stepped out
and headed left down a long corridor.

"Don't take it personally if it seems
she's angry with you – that's a way she gets
from time to time, no matter who's around.
It's sound and fury, signifying…well,
no one knows just what it signifies,
or who she's telling off. She likes to yell."

The corridor was brightly lit; they walked
for what seemed like a long time. Then they stopped
before a white door with a child's loud drawing:
a bunch of daisies, pinned into the door
at eye level, brown and yellow crayons.

"Did she have a child that drew this for her?"
he asked.

"Oh no, she never had a child.
This was a niece. She's had it here a while."

He worked the lock and opened up the door
into a darkened, gray, and empty room.
Nothing moved to register their presence.

"She must be on the sun deck. It's this way,"
the squat attendant said, and motioned right.
After a few more ages in the maze
they came out onto a yellow deck.
A slatted white chair faced away from them,
and she too was turned, eyeing the long
expanse of green which rolled away, down to
a small pond and a straight line of birches.
She wore the kind of white hat women used
for gardening; it kept her face from sight
until they'd drawn up even with her chair.

And there she was. At first she didn't see
him. He studied how her face had changed;
it was more angular and drawn, and she
kept shaking her head back and forth as though
she was refusing something, and repeating
what she wanted, saying *"Carolina,
Carolina ... all the lies, all of
the lies ... ,"* her words as though recited, wistful.
Then suddenly she turned her head to look
at him, and shouted *"You know what you did!"*

"There, there, Carol, don't you know your friend?
He's come to see you," the attendant said,
his voice a soothing thread to bring her back.
But she would not be comforted.

"You know!"
she said, and turned her head away from him.
*"Carolina ... all the lies ... all of
the lies ..."* Her voice trailed off. She seemed to settle
once again into her quiet study
   of close cut green and birches over water.

11

He reached the house again two mornings later.
The banana colored bug was parked
out on the street. He'd tried, but couldn't think
of anywhere to go besides back here.
The window box blooms rustled in the breeze
as he passed by and started up the steps
that led him to her door. This time he knew
what lay beyond it was a different place
from what he'd been so sure he'd find at first.
He thought he knew just how it would be different;
in fact, when the door opened he was met
by her familiar, knowing face, unsmiling.

They sat out in the living room. He took
the couch, she took the chair of kendall green.
There seemed to be no motion in the room
as he tried to explain why he'd come back.
In a weekend shirt and jeans, she drew her

knees up together sideways in the chair
and looked so somber that he paused before
describing his encounter with the past
and how he'd gotten both an answer and
a host of other questions for his trouble.

Her forehead smooth, her kind and steady eyes
combined to show him that it made no difference
what he said. Nothing he said would move her.
Yet she listened carefully and let
him speak; nothing about her was forbidding.

"What I felt with you, that's what I wanted.
What I want, I mean," he said, and stopped.

Her smile was rueful, and her voice the sigh
of one who's just put down a heavy box.

"When I was her to you, I had her power.
As long as you believed, I could accept
you in her name, and give you what you needed.
But just as soon as you lost your illusion —
and when was that, the morning, or the night
before? I thought so. After that *I* had
no power at all, as her or as myself."

Behind the patient hollow of her voice
he heard the scrambled sound of children shouting
distantly as they played in the park.
Her closer voice, as though explaining to
a child, went regularly up and down.

"Once you *knew* and let me play the role,

I felt it was a kind of violation."

He hung his head. "I should have realized,"
he looked back up and said. "I wasn't fair.
I wanted what you gave me, but from her."

"So you went on and left me, and discovered
she can't ever give you what you want,"
she summarized, as he could not have done
as cleanly, or with such an even temper.

"Yes," he said,"but how did you know that?"

This time she managed a wry smile. "That's easy.
If she could, you wouldn't have come back."
He felt a distance open up between them,
and he forgot to hear the outside shouting.

"But I had it, everything I want,
here, from you."

                    The distance grew no less.

"You don't know me at all," she said. "We'd have
to start over again as almost-strangers,
and forget what's happened. I can't do that.
Sorry."

       He saw that nothing he could do
or say to her would bring her any closer.
Disconsolate, he let his head hang down;
she was no longer moved to comfort him.

11

*I should have known, but hadn't thought that he'd
be back. In the few days that he was gone
the daily pace of life again took over,
and sitting by myself in silent rooms
has made the whole encounter seem unreal.
The memory of his caresses made
my skin crawl, so I showered too
frequently and scrubbed with heavy towels.
When the quiet was too much I listened
to the cello suites, losing myself
in Bach sung through the deep tone of Casals,
proving emotion lives outside of time.*

*Why has this narrow soul appeared to me?
And what am I to learn from our exchange?"*

.

She closed the journal, went into the kitchen,
and started making lemon tea. The water
needed time; she put on the Fifth Suite,
the one whose Sarabande had always helped her.
Rare in having not one double stop,
it made her hear the hidden colors change
with every turn of solo melody,
and every time she heard them differently.

Sipping her tea, both hands around a mug,
she thought of her condition. Like Kim Novak
in *Vertigo*, she'd struggled in a trap,
forced to turn into what she had been,
a pretender caught in her pretending.
"No," she said, "not forced – I volunteered.

What *was* it about him that made me do it?"

She put down the empty mug, turned off
the music as the 1st Gavotte began,
got ready to go out. She told herself
"His vision was so strong, I couldn't fight it.
No, that's not true. I chose to be that woman.
What she meant to him was more, and different,
than I had ever meant to anyone.
The chance to be *her* – it was just too tempting."

She put on her rough-textured, wheat colored
coat and a light wool cranberry scarf.

"No, not *Vertigo* – it's more the story
of the chambermaid who's asked to give
herself to the new husband in the dark
by his reluctant bride. Relieved although
the bride might be, she envies still the maid
for standing in the full light of desire.
Yes, that's better. And it was the way,
the *only* way for me to feel the full
force of that unfinished man's desire."

She walked then down the hall, passing the paintings
that she'd worked on for years, the early ones
there to show one can't be tentative;
then to the living room, where looking down,
framed and luminous, they showed her colors,
the ones he'd been too fixed on her to notice.

"Will he go back now to his family?"
she thought as she stepped lightly on the porch.

"I don't know him well enough to guess,"
she realized, and shook her head. "So I
suppose I'll have to be the one to learn
from this peculiar, painful interlude. Remain
yourself, for starters. Stay away from men
who are obsessed by any other woman.
When the crisis comes, don't choose to lie.
Funny, I thought I was too old for that —
thought I knew better. And maybe I did.
Didn't do better, though, and that's what counts."

She walked off, past the window boxes still
holding their bloom, now deeper in the season.

Falling Asleep

At night when lying on my back in bed
I fold my hands, first one way, then another:
knit up my fingers, left hand first, then right;
or lay one palm down flat against the other's
back, then switch, and think about the change
in how the different figurations feel.

While all are mostly similar, the subtle
settling of the crossing bones, and shifting
surfaces of skin, though unimportant,
occupy my mind with differences,
and slowly open up the way to sleep.

They have until tonight, that is – tonight
the differences point me back awake,
and put me on a wonder of the night
when one will feel exactly like another.

Finishing the Almond Crescent

After you've dispatched the almond crescent,
watching it grow smaller with each bite,
crackled its slivered nuts, its chewy core,
blonde on blondness, seeing nothing else,

your eyes drop to the bottom of the dish,
where several crumbs stand pale against the blue.
You lick your fingertip, and bring it down.
They stick to it; you lift it to your tongue.

Like these years in old age, after you
have given up expecting more to come,
they are more afterthought than memory
but still retain the taste of what is gone.

from *me & the Originator*

1. The Trunk

It's a good thing that I found that trunk.
I thought it was to store my seventy-eights,
but what was hidden in it changed my life.
Just when the record company was on
us to record originals instead
of covers, and the guys all looked to me –
and I had nothing. Not a clue about
how to write a song – with words at least.
I knew a lot of chords, and had a million
riffs I could pull out, but what to say,
and how to do it? I was at a loss.

So when I found the papers in the bottom
of that ancient wooden trunk, and read 'em,
that pulled me – all of us – out of the fire.
I had questions; that stack had the answers.
Old and yellow, maybe, but to me
they were pure gold. And we all got rich,
although we all got shafted, and split up,
and most of them went broke, but that was later.
While it lasted, there was lots to go
around. I never told 'em where I got
the words, and I felt guilty about that.

But nowhere on those pages was it written
whose words they were. Just poems, you might say,
or maybe there'd been music too, but not written
down anywhere. I put the music on,

and we went in and cut 'em, and the people
must have liked it. We got pretty famous
for a while there. When reporters used
to pester me about the songs, I'd say
"Shoot, the words are all around us in
the air, I don't ask questions, I just write
'em down." And that was fairly true, in fact.

Whoever wrote them had some kind of life,
if it wasn't just some story. I'd look through
that stack of pages – it was like he read
my mind sometimes (or she, you never know).
Seemed like I lived those stories, though they weren't
in any order. As the years went by
I'd get into some kind of situation,
and sure enough, there'd be a page about it.
It got so I would wonder which was next,
and hope that others were a long way off.
Near the end it got uncomfortable.

2. What He Carried

As early as I could, I ran away
from home, and carried everything I left
behind. There was no reason to look back:
I didn't have to follow it to know
the line of blood led to the witch's house.
I'd left a drop at every other step.
She knew exactly where to strike, and how
to use her cold words like a spur of ice.
So intimate it was, I held the wound,
after they pierced me, in, as blood ran out.

Hard as the wind blew rain as I approached
the river I was fearful of the currents,
both air and water; so as not to be
swept off I loaded stones in every pocket
and tried the ford; soon in over my head,
I learned how to press on, holding my breath.

3. Useless Good Advice

"Sure," he said, "it's okay for a hobby.,
but you need something steady, see? And there's
a lot of jobs that you'd be good at. Think about
a trade where you can use your hands, and maybe
be outdoors, you'd like that, and you're handy."

He was trying, and he meant well, but
he was talking to the son he thought I was,
not me. My life was never any kind
of steady. Never had a normal job
I didn't quit within a week. I had to play,
that's all – never really had a choice.

Found some guys who thought the way I did,
jammed into a Fairlane Ford and pulled
a trailer with our amps and instruments
wedged in with a PA and some speakers,
and dragged around until we found some folks
who let us set up in a corner on
the floor of some dark bar, and pass the hat.

Later we'd play for the door. We had
a Chevy van by then, with a partition

and blown out shocks, and we would travel
anyplace that we could get to, play,
and make it back home while it was still dark.
As long as we had time each day away
from each other, we could make it work.

After we had made it, what they called
making it at least, we stayed out on
the road for months, which made us want to kill
each other; that close just ain't natural.

What wore you down was getting to the job,
and, after, getting paid and getting home.
The playing part was why we kept it going;
when even that became work, we broke up.

4. Self-Reliance

They tell this story about Rube, the lefty
Rube Waddell, who ended his career
in Nineteen-Ten. No man alive has seen
him pitch. I think I know, though, how he felt.
The band quit on me once, in Cincinnati,
before the gig. Not one of them showed up.
Club owner didn't want to pay me, said
he hired a band and I was just a solo.
Said I couldn't hold the crowd. I said
"just watch and learn," and went on by myself.
Told the crowd up front what happened, said
"I'm gonna do this set all by my lonesome,
and you're gonna love it." Killed 'em, and
he had to pay up. While he counted out the money,

real slow, like he couldn't bear to let
it leave his hands, he made a face just like
the one Rube's skipper must have had that day.

5. The Bee's Lot

What makes this blossom stand out to the bee?
Is it a matter of proximity,
some subtle color only he can see,
or some nuance of scent that he can feel?

A factor finally quickening today
deeply embedded in the DNA,
emerging to the surface in a way
that, unaware, the blossom can't conceal?

To near, helpless before the mystery
of what has chosen blossom for the bee;
to taste, believing that his choice is free
is the bee's lot, yet the nectar's real.

6. What He Deserved

He had some habits that were hard to break.
He handled money every night. I should
have known. But we'd come up together, been
through everything, the times we had to split
one hot dog five ways. I trusted him.

Sure, once we took off I made royalties
from publishing and writing, but then I

provided all the songs. The paperwork
was in my name, and when the taxmen came
and popped us seven figures for unpaid
taxes, no one made a move but me –
I bailed them out and paid it off in full,
and never asked how we got in the hole.

When I went solo, I felt bad at first
I didn't take him with me, so I let
them keep the band name, make the best of it.
Then they went straight down on their own. At first
nobody understood how they could go
so broke so fast, and I got criticized
for leaving them behind. Most people thought
they would have been okay if I had stayed.
So later when we found out he'd been skimming
gate receipts for years, I felt betrayed.
I didn't talk about it; we'd been friends.
But everything he went through after that,
he had it coming to him all along.

7. Learn to Draw!

When I first saw her in the last page ad
while finishing a DC comic book,
I didn't know what I was looking at.
"Learn to Draw!" it said, and there she was,

a fashionable beauty in a wrap,
hand-drawn in lines, but young and flawless-looking,
with a feather in her hair. I liked
to look at her but didn't think much of it.

Then one day, all at once, I saw the crone:
withered, dry lips drawn tight – optical
illusion, flipping from the beauty to
the crone according to the way you looked.

"Pictographic Ambiguity,"
so called. Some claimed to see them both together;
for me, the beauty fled at once, like milk
which curdled in the bottle overnight,

and after that the crone was there alone,
declaring the true face of the young model,
reminding me how hard it was for her
to be as beautiful as she appeared.

8. Breaking Up is Hard to Do

This is just the way some people roll.
You grab the wire, and if the juice is on,
you can't let go, it's out of your control.
You're burning up, but your will power's gone.

I caught this more than once when I was young.
The drama was like living in a thriller.
One kept showing off a borrowed gun;
I wised up when she wanted me to kill her.

It seems like almost everyone I know
has got into this rut sometime or other.
You feel like every kind of dope, although
you shouldn't. Every fool is like another.

You're human. You were born to take the fall.
Maybe blues is universal, after all.

9. Who Owns It?

Coming from the hundred-plus degrees
of the sun-punished downtown square, the air
conditioning inside the jewelry store
refreshed me like a pool plunge, instantly.

My band was still out playing, backing up
a singer from South Africa whose rhythm
section got held up en route. Forever
looking for an extra taste, they all
agreed to stay out on the griddle for
another set in all that blinding heat.
I wasn't needed, so I lunged away
and found the cold spot that the festival
promoters had provided for the bands:
cool jewels and a local microbrew.

I saw him as an icy swallow danced
its way down, chilling every inch. I felt
the liquid sluice, delicious, and he smiled,
standing over by a diamond case.
I figured he was from another act,
but he was from another place entirely.
"You're So-and-So," he said, "I follow you.
I know a lot about you." And he started
talking like I knew him, like we'd grown
up together, telling me about
my life: I did this, I did that, I went

here, and after that . . . He told me things
about myself that even I'd forgotten.
I wasn't going back out in that heat,
so I put up with it. He didn't seem
dangerous, just hopelessly obsessed.
I just wished he hadn't picked on me.

He never seemed to tire of telling me
about myself. He said "The first song on
your last album, was that about your wife –
the first one – how she left you for your bass
player in the middle of a tour?"
"Sure," I said, "you've got me figured out."

That made his day; he kept on happily,
and I thought if he only knew the truth –
I don't know who that was written about,
I just put some music to it. He'd
run with it from there, like they all did.

But later on I thought some more about it.
That lyric was about the way I felt,
the first couple of years after she left.
If I could write, I could've written it.
It made it so I felt like singing it,
like I owned a little bit of it,
like anybody would who felt like that.
So maybe he was right. It took some years,
but I got over it. It took more years
to find a bassist good as Sam had been.
She kept him off the road; they're still together.
That's how it was with us, one or the other.

10. Solo

After you go solo, nothing stays
the same. You still need help to keep it going;
there's too much on your shoulders otherwise,
and any good team lets you be your best.

But you're not equals like you used to be;
now they're just employees, and you're the boss.
It's your name out front, you take the risk.
They come and go, and they're all at your mercy.

If they want their jobs, they stay in line.
But they stay together, and they talk
behind your back. There's always some resentment.
Your face is in the lights, they're on the margin.

But you get used to being isolated;
there's comfort at the center of attention.
You get so good at going it alone,
in fact, you can forget you started out

relieved to have the company of equals,
facing the common trials for the same reason.
What hardens in you then can make you pass
on every other kind of company:

The future likely will be like the past;
what probably won't work's not worth the effort.
You've learned to trust relying on yourself.
Living alone trains you to keep your distance.

11. Young and Old

It's said the old will not sort with the young:
what's been already; what is yet to come.
Faith creaks with every step across the floor;
doubt tries the sills and locks at every door.

Differing desires need different tending,
one eye on the beginning, one the ending.
How to share a world one is conceiving
daily, which another thinks of leaving?

Before me, after you, time has its turn,
declaring if we two will have to learn
to hurry through too early or too late
one opening, the other closing, gate.

12. Confessing the Blues

Whoever wrote that could have read my mind,
but not when I first read it. I had risen
at no one's expense: I'd yet to rise,
not having put those words to proper use.

My luck had not yet run to good; I'd reached
no promised land. I'd eyed it from across
the tracks, from the dry place where I began.
I hadn't even started being wrong.

But as the years went on, and I dug deep
into the sheaf of paper I'd discovered,

I came to be the teller of that tale
whose life was indistinguishable from it.

Seeing it at first, I had no notion
of the kind of guilt it spoke about,
nor did I know how I would come to feel it,
a sentence no confession could commute.

13. How It Goes

You work throughout your life to become strong,
so those you care about can be protected.
You hold them close to keep them from the wrong,
far from any injustices suspected.

A day comes when the strength you counted on
begins to fail you, like it knows you're due.
Your closest friends drift off then, mounted on
whatever distances themselves from you.

Once it starts to go, I find it strange
spending what amounts to my last days
finding how to take what I can't change.
It isn't right, but that's the way it stays.

His Neighbor's Take

When Jesus came around, you notice how
he didn't go complaining all the time
about what sinners we all are? Instead
he talked about the way we ought to be.

He drove the moneychangers from the Temple,
sure – gouging worshippers for temple coins
and doves for offerings was robbery.
Done in the house of prayer just made it worse.

I'll tell you why he withered up the fig tree.
From a distance, it looked like it had
a load of figs, when it was just a sham.
Jesus was big on being what you seem.

He wasn't changing water into wine,
except his mother asked him to. It wasn't
showing off, he did it for a favor,
and said it was against his better judgment.

He fed the multitudes a couple times,
but that's because those people stayed to hear him.
It got too late to walk back home for dinner.
He was nothing if not practical.

He got that from his dad, the carpenter.
When he put in a crossbeam, it stayed put.
He was a builder, not a tearer-downer,
except the times you have to, to start over.

All that curing and the casting out
of demons, those were people needed help.
And bringing back the dead, he did that for
the families. Family meant a lot to him.

I think he could have come down from that cross,
if he wanted to. He must have stayed
up there for a reason. Like I said,
he was a very level-headed guy.

Holding My Breath

That was some breath I took when I was ten,
deep in the back seat of our Pontiac,
riding with my parents down Route 1
to our vacation week in Florida. .

I meant to show my body who was boss
and hold that breath as long as possible,
and finally worked it up to two full minutes,
trying all the while to go unnoticed.

But giving in at last, I started up
again the ins and outs that, ever since
the smack that got me started, had run on
through every gasp of fear and gulp for air.

This welcoming the world with every breath,
this exhalation that makes room for more,
are always with me, though they go unmarked.
It's breathing that's the boss; I should remember.

The lesson is repeated which I try
so hard not to learn: for all I take
into myself, so close and intimate
they couldn't be more mine, there has to be,
to make a place for more, a letting go.

How I Learned About Attraction

A button, and an acorn, and two washers;
a piece of yarn I found under the couch –
I saved them all for my experiment.

I got a broken radio, and pried
the magnet from behind the speaker cone.
Put it near my compass. It went haywire.

It stuck to parts of the refrigerator
door, but fell off other parts. I tried
a nail that stuck to it, then one that didn't.

The button and the other stuff did nothing.
Food and drink, like milk, were not affected.
Thumbtacks it picked up, but pushpins, no.

Nothing I did could change what it attracted,
or what it wouldn't. That was magnetism.
I accepted it for what it was.

Later, when I went to school, some kids
I liked, and wanted to be near. But most
of them had no effect on me at all.

And of the ones I liked, some acted just
as if they were a button or an acorn.
To some who liked me, I was only yarn.

I didn't see a similarity
to how it was when nails met up with magnets.

Then my experiments with love took over.

I came up with a lot of reasons why
this one I wanted couldn't love me back,
while that one couldn't make me feel a twinge.

As a kid I'd learned about attraction,
that mystery you just had to accept.
But when I grew up, I forgot I knew it.

How I Learned About Blindness

Inexplicably, his face untroubled,
my best friend's little brother stood atop
a pile of blown out tires left of the entrance
to the truck barn where my father's men
housed their plows and tree-cutting equipment.

He held his head dead even with a row
of windows which extended on both sides
behind him, patient as we older boys
picked up the rocks. The game we'd just invented
was Miss-His-Head-But-Still-Break-All-The-Windows.

An almost wholly unsupported trust
buoyed up his grin as we took careful aim,
and we were likewise blindly confident.
We chucked the rocks. The shatter of the glass
was such a hollow, satisfying sound.

When more than sixty years had passed, I asked
if he remembered how he'd felt, and why
he'd done it. He admitted sheepishly
that to this day he couldn't understand;
it must have been "stone cold stupidity."

And yet blind trust and confidence had both
been vindicated: one undamaged boy,
one bank of windows broken. How did Fate
not crush us all for tempting it so rashly?
For one time only, blindness was a charm.

How I Learned About Parenting

At four I got away with stealing cream,
or so I thought. That had to be the year —
when I was five we left the tenement
and moved out to the park, all by ourselves;
that house had a milk box with a cover.

But when my family lived in the apartment,
the creaking of the milkman on the stairs
up to the second floor would wake me up,
and I would tiptoe by the bedroom door
and make sure that my parents were asleep.

New light was coming through the kitchen window,
so I could see the cut glass of the doorknob,
and use both hands to turn it noiselessly.
There on the floor outside the opened door
I'd kneel before the slim and graceful bottle.

The milk back then was whole and separated,
and cold from standing in the empty hallway.
It was protected by a paper lid
inside the glass mouth, like a Dixie cup,
and covered by a waxy paper cap,

held on by folded flaps around the rim.
I'd use my fingernail to pick one free,
and ease it open, just enough to loosen
and remove the cover. Then the tab
had to be pried and pulled to lift the lid.

I knew the tasty cream was on the top,
its color pure, like in the catechism
where white milk in the bottle represented
the spotless soul when in a state of grace.
And I would drink a little, not too much.

Then I'd replace the lid, and putting on
the cap, I'd press the loose flap back again.
And no one ever mentioned it. As though
no one could tell the quart was less than full,
as though no one could know that it was me.

How I Learned About Supply and Demand

AIT, Ft. Leonard Wood, MO – September 1970

When the storm hit, we were at the range;
in fact, my squad was on the firing line.
The rain came down so fast we didn't have
our ponchos on, and so we all got soaked.

They told us to keep firing, while the rest
of the trainees took shelter underneath
a nearby plywood shell. They stood there dry
while we were firing, prone and getting doused.

The ammunition kept on coming. Once
we were as wet as we could get, they had
us break out ponchos. The Missouri heat
burned right through the rain. Our ponchos steamed.

Every now and then a lefty jumped
up off the line and danced around. Ejected
casings flipped off to the right, and found
their scalding way down to the shooter's neck.

When the rain refused to let up, we were told
to just keep firing on the automatic
setting. What we hit was not important.
The barrels of our M-16s were smoking.

After a half an hour, we had spent
the ammunition quota of the day.

They brought us off the line and marched us back.
When we eleven men turned in our weapons,

the heat had melted out the rifling
inside the bores. Those weapons now were useless;
they issued us new ones; I found out later
ammunition couldn't be returned.

They told me 50,000 rounds were due
tomorrow at the range. Where they were stored
there wasn't room for any unspent bullets.
As for the men, we were already wet.

How I Learned About Time

After listening carefully to Pops
and wondering where he got those solos from –
after a lifetime's listening and playing,
putting the notes he chose into the order
that he used, and at the proper time,

to figure how those phrases came to him,
studying the accents on the one
and three he had the saxes set for him
on all those Thirties Luis Russell sides,
remembering what Ruby said about it:

"When you're in two, you think in four;
when you're in four, you think in two,"
I still was puzzled how the hell he did it –
how he thought to start and stop those phrases
where he did, the way he felt the time.

After a few more years I realized
how much he had to know to play that way.
To make a phrase more like a melody
you had to know the chords inside and out
and play not so much on as over them.

On the unissued take of "Swing That Music"
done with Jimmy Dorsey, after all
those high Ds on the one, he syncopates
some phrases in defiance of the time
that for decades left me in confusion.

When to play, with each note giving way,
and how to tell when each led to another?
I felt a little somersault each time
I heard it, deep below my solar plexus,
and couldn't tell when the next note was coming.

I must have listened to it fifty times,
and tried to figure it a hundred ways;
my body simply couldn't process it.
Then it happened – without even trying,
I suddenly could feel the way to play it.

Like waking up one day and finding out
you knew the way to wiggle your left ear
after a lifetime when you never could.
And now it wasn't even hard to do –
but no one could have ever told you how.

How I Learned to Love Mozart

In music, I preferred at first the more
dramatic gestures: Mozart didn't speak
to me the way Beethoven did. I granted
that the fault was mine, and I was missing

a whole world of expression others prized.
But just as in the eye, I felt the heart
could have a blind spot to a kind of greatness
plainly clear to anybody else.

*

When I first met the girl, I didn't know
that lately she'd committed to, and been
thrown over by, the great love of her life.
Stunned, she stayed behind; he went away.

For months we spent a lot of time together.
She warmed to me, and I became convinced
in time I didn't want to live without her.
Then he returned and said he'd been mistaken.

Could they go back to how it was before,
and move away together as they'd planned?
She admitted when she spoke to me
her heart was torn, but what to do about it?

I told her she could never be with me
the way I wanted, until she was free

of what she'd had with him; that she should go,
and live with him, and give it every chance.

We agreed that it would take a year
at least for her to know if it was right,
and that we shouldn't be in touch at all.
I promised I would spend the year alone.

All that year I accepted day by day
the arrows of emotion piercing me.
I exposed my heart, and ceaselessly
they found it out. But not to magnify

their power, I made no attempt to struggle.
I let them pass on through, as though they were
those particles to whom mass is as nothing.
I felt no pain, but I was being changed.

When after a year I learned that she
was to be married, I could let it go;
I'd lasted through the harrowing, and so
I felt that I was ready to move on.

*

One day I listened to the "Dissonant"
quartet, which opens with a strange
disjointed passage, as though every part
is posing both a question and an answer.

Musing on a troubling in the heart,
it drifts as though the mood will never lift.

Yet twenty two bars later, like the sun
streaming though the clouds, a melody

emerges, simple joy in a clear voice,
buoying the spirit. Suddenly my feelings
opened up, and I met Mozart, soul
to soul – a lifelong source of consolation.

How It Happens

The door into the next room of your dream
isn't there until you open it.

I Fall While Running

Near the beginning of my seventieth year,
during a workout, finishing my jogging,
easing on the final stretch of miles,
relaxed into the pace, I pick it up
last lap, and push my way around the track.

Going at a decent clip, I make
the turn into the straightaway, and catch
my toe against the carpet, breaking stride.
I try to right myself as I tilt to
the left, but though I struggle through my leg
I can't correct the list, and over seven strides
slip increments, as though I were a bulging
droplet, hanging from the faucet rim
and losing purchase. So I choose to fall,
and let the track slam up to meet my knee,
my shoulder, and my face, a rolling move
not broken by my hands, but punctuated
at full stop when my head smacks on the floor.

I pick myself back up by pushing pieces
at sharp angles to the carpet, first
my left leg, then right arm. I am not broken;
I have fallen well. Still, since I've come
into my seventieth year, it will be two
months uneven healing, when it would
have been two weeks just twenty years ago.
I'll play the model patient, anyway,
but don't mistake the warning: though you do
all that will and effort can to cheat
time at the game, you do so at your peril.

In Service of the Word

for David Cashman

1

We all had a favorite high school teacher;
take a moment to remember yours.
What made her or him so different?
I'd bet that they share a lot in common.
They liked their students, and they loved their jobs.
They knew their subjects cold, inside and out.
But that was just the first part of the story.

They paid attention to you, learned about you,
enough to know what motivated you,
if you responded to a gentle push
or outright challenge. They were always fair,
and they could tell from looking at your face
how well prepared you were for class each day,
and how to ask a question you could answer,
instead of showing everyone how much
you didn't know. You felt them on your side.

And they remembered that you were in high school,
no finished product, and a dozen things
in your life every day felt more important
than anything that they assigned to you.
The days when buckling down wasn't enough,
they knew that all young walkers are at first
unsteady on their feet. They'd let you wobble,
but reached out if you looked about to fall,

took extra time to help you if you asked,
and offered when you couldn't find the words.

Now English might not be your favorite subject,
but English teachers often are the ones
that we remember best, because they got
to teach more than the language; they taught life.
Atticus and Scout, Polonius
and Hamlet – characters who felt and acted
in familiar ways, who made their choices
and lived with consequences. If you weren't
preoccupied with being in your teens,
and had the time and inclination,
Literature showed you other worlds
and gave you things to think about.
And maybe now you read for your own pleasure,
and make time to enrich your inner life.

2

Now let's take a look behind the curtain.
What's life like for a teacher? If the school
is independent, then the day is longer,
the pay is shorter, and the classes smaller.
You choose it for a better chance to teach,
to get to know your students well enough
to help them find their way, learn how to work,
not slide because they hide out in a crowd,
not feel that no one knows or cares about them.
It is a servant's role; you choose to serve.
You're often asked to do a little more;
you steal time from your private life, and yet

you never feel you're doing all you can.
When there's a problem, you can't take for granted
that parents will agree to take your side;
sometimes you will be treated as a servant,
not an equal – and you chose to serve.

And every time you're seen or heard, you're teaching.
Not just in class, not just your subject; children
are watching, listening, learning if you tell
the truth, make good on promises or threats,
if you're a phony or a hypocrite,
happy to see them or afraid to face them –
if you always act like the adult
that you're supposed to be; what you believe,
and if you live up to your level of belief.

They watch us all the time, the children do,
to see new ways of being an adult.
That happens everywhere. But teachers take
responsibility for what they're teaching.
All day and every day you have the chance
to do some good, to do great harm. The role
must be accepted, carried out down to
the letter, all the time we're seen or heard,
and there are moments every day when we
can help or hurt a child with just a word:
say the right one and they open out;
say the wrong one and you feel them crumple
in. That damaged look will haunt you, and
you long to find a way to make it right.
Most days you take on faith you're doing good
that in some future season will bear fruit,
though you may not be privileged to see.

Some days you feel your efforts are in vain.
But however much you need to see
your students making progress, you must keep
that need to yourself. It's hard enough
for them to grow without your putting more
weight on their shoulders. Want them to improve,
but for their sake, and never for your own.
The teacher's needs are not part of the role.

It has its difficulties, this profession.

3

So now we come to David Harold Cashman,
"Doc" in our youth, just David when I met
him in his teens, and here at Country Day
for thirty eight years he's embraced the role
of Mister Cashman. He's been larger than
that role, but he has always played it to
the scale appropriate. Here is a worthy model.

He loved the word, and taught the use of language:
writing, reading, listening and speaking.
Good writing puts our thoughts in single file,
to lead ourselves and others on a clear
path, not drifting off in all directions;
good reading lets us see the world beyond
the page, the true intentions of the writer;
good listening and speaking let us have
a chance to influence and learn from others.
He did the teacher's job, and went beyond:
he showed another way to be adult.

You knew his values though he didn't preach them;
you saw them in the way he treated people.
He was patient with your errors, he was pleased
with your accomplishments, for your own sake.
He gave you chances; he was slow to judge.
He gave you the respect we all deserve
before expecting any of it back.
He found time for you, and he really listened.
He did the things that all great teachers do.
He did it all, and never seemed hard pressed.

We Italians call that sprezzatura,
the difficult accomplished with a grace
that speaks of ease where nothing won is easy,
nothing done without a sacrifice.
For all who choose to serve in this pursuit,
more profession than a job, and more
a calling than profession, sacrifice
is daily bread. For those with families
life spent in service to loved ones at home
is simply life. For those who serve at work,
you have a second family. Like the first
it gets your best attention. Every one
of us who's waited with a student, last to be
picked up after a late away game, as
the parking lot gets dark, and making sure
his ride has come before you leave yourself,
knows what it's all about. You're the adult;
you show up and you stay. You live the role,
though you may be the last one fed that night.

Like so many others, David had
these two families, and met their needs

before he took time for himself. That's not
unusual. But as I said, he's more
than Mister Cashman, teaching how to use
the word; he has a talent with the word,
a writer's skill to manifest a poet's
soul. His fiction and his poetry
are versions of the world as filtered through
his sensibility. They never shout;
they keep their balance even as the floor
is heaving underfoot. Collected, calmly
spiritual, they will find an order
when it seems that nothing's making sense.
He has, in short, a message for our times.

When the *New Yorker* published his short story
in the early Eighties, it appeared
much more would follow. But his students got
his best time and energy. He wrote
on weekends, over summers; though it was
for a noble reason, he wrote less.

An artist's life can seem a selfish one
because you have to meet another need;
you find you have another mouth to feed
that lives down at the center of your being
and hounds you day and night with its demands.
It is your deepest self, your most insistent
master, the one you are compelled to serve
on pain of losing touch with who you are.
A need like breathing; you can hold your breath,
but not forever. Putting others first
postpones the day you satisfy that need.

So up to now he hasn't written all
he could have if his day job had been less
demanding; from now on I wish him all
the time he needs to fully serve his talent.
He's put the role of Mister Cashman down;
as David Harold Cashman, he has wealth
to give us in the currency of words.

Beyond the teacher's and the writer's word
there is another, where he draws his strength.
This is a man who in ripe middle age
went back to school to study Greek, to read
a language one step closer to that word,
the Word in the beginning of the Book
of John, the Word that Paul carried around
and spread throughout the ancient world.
It isn't hard to say the Word, but few
truly commit themselves to living by it;
that takes a change of heart. That he has made
his heart a servant to the Word is there
in everything he says and does, in how
he models what it means to be a human,
treating others as they should be treated.
It is the simple secret that explained him,
before he took the role of Mister Cashman,
all through his service here at Country Day,
and now, after his last class, going forward.
Consider what he keeps on teaching. In
a dark time, we are much in need of learning.

In the Fourth Quarter

Off they go and out they go, some dead,
some spinning into madness, or betrayed
by body parts or functions. Through the day
some catechize their pain in an array
of questions; answers range from venial
to mortal, like the sins they once committed
but having since forgotten, can't confess,
and so their bodies don't know to forgive.

So many flavors in the taste of pain!
It doesn't satisfy, like guilt, which they
at least know they deserve. After a youth
when hurt was rare and barely filling, now
it tops them off and sees they're amply fed,
and promises to never leave them hungry.

In the Later Rounds

Numb from medication side effects,
my fingertips can't feel the buttonhole.
The button jumps away each time I try
 to bring the two together at my neck.

Before the button finds the buttonhole,
my arms are stiff and painful at the crooks
from holding up my hands under my chin
too long. I let them dangle down to rest.

Astonished at myself, I'm learning how
I have to concentrate to do the things
that always came to me so easily.
I bargain hard for every victory.

In my unending struggle with the world,
there are as many targets as before,
but the essential question is no longer
do I strike often, but do I strike true?

Joy to the World

Christmas 2019

The sky is overcast tonight
and any doings overhead
which might shed a celestial light
are walled off by dark clouds instead.

Some claim that angel voices clear
ring out above the local din,
but most of us can only hear
the sound of neighbors quarreling.

Since not one simple word of love
can get through to us from above,
for us to feel the joy again,
we'll have to find the word within.

Kingdom of Despair

This dark star risen over me
blots itself up in such a way
that none can see how utterly
it cancels out the light of day.

And night has fallen through the world
so deeply that this globe of light
and warmth in which I live and breathe
is all that can protect my sight.

I'm hopeful, keeping calm and bright,
but will the candle last the night
while cracks that form above my head
are letting in the dark instead?

Krazy Kat and Junk on the Moon

July 20, 2019

Fifty years ago tonight
the moon a cat was looking at
was altered in its fitful light
by someone's finally looking back.

The Sunday strip of *Krazy Kat*
showed, fifty years before that date,
Ignatz asleep on a landscape flat
beneath a moon immaculate.

This moon still manages to light us
despite the bits of bric-a-brac
we left. It's spoiled by that detritus;
we'll never have our old moon back.

That spoon-without-a-handle moon
will look on Kat and Mouse and men,
and trill unspoiled its lunar tune,
when fifty years have passed again.

Light Breaks In

My eyes don't pace as deeply in the trench
of words arranged in lines along the page
as they once did, although in their defense
they've soldiered on from childhood into age,

and served reliably without complaint.
Until just recently, that is, for now
they skip from place to place without restraint
like stones across a pond, and don't allow

the words to keep original intent.
And yet I find my mind supplies a clue
to meaning different from what others meant:
repeatedly, new words are breaking through.

I learn now, not from what was really said,
but from the messages I think I read.

Living in the Future

Sea level's shifted underneath your feet.
Magnetic north is drifting from the pole.
You used to lean on answers that repeat;
no old key now fits any new keyhole.

Your problems will admit no diminution.
Stumbling blocks will be put in your way.
Don't fall in love with any one solution;
what worked yesterday won't work today.

It used to be you'd spend your life to find
security and a safe place to rest.
That's out the window. Now retrain your mind
to grapple with a different daily test.

Let go whatever got you through before.
Change direction when you hit a wall
instead of looking for a hidden door.
To rest is no security at all.

Slip around the obstacles you meet;
go in the way you're being made to go,
even when it looks like a retreat.
The right path may be not for you to know.

At rest is good as dead, so let that be
and move. Be water flowing to the sea.

Naming Rights

When God first spoke to Adam, He
used words as clear as they could be,
and set him on the heady game
of giving everything a name.

And Adam didn't need a school
to understand the only rule
God gave him; all the words made sense
except the one for consequence.

They didn't have a word for sin
until the serpent butted in
and uttered what we call a lie.
"Go, eat," he said, "you will not die."

Half-true – for in a way, they didn't,
strictly speaking – but half-hidden,
until the act had made them see
the death-word hanging on the tree.

Usurping Adam's power to brand,
the serpent turned it to his hand:
whoever acted in a fit
would find there was a word for it.

The unnamed act was never heard
until Cain coined the murder-word
by doing it. As others tried,
vocabulary multiplied,

and dark words blurred the antecedent
language, once so clear in Eden.
So speech intended to deceive
was brought to bear on all since Eve.

And other evils came of it
once words could name their opposite.
Soon everyone was seeing how
half-truths and untruths clog the bough.

Still new words grew, both good and dire
as different motives would inspire.
With names a second language Babel,
how to distinguish fact from fable?

By their fruits so shall you know
them, after they've had time to grow;
as always it's a human fate
to see the truth once it's too late.

Today we need to understand
each other more than ever, yet
so much is serpent-speak. Can we
now tell the death-words on the tree?

New Year's Eve

December 31, 2018

I sing a song for what has been,
and one for what will be;
for time which brings and takes away
and keeps rewriting me.

For all that I remember right
that lasts through every version;
for all I hoped to throw away
returned after excursion.

My manuscript is not complete,
and undergoes revision;
grant me a fresh blank page or two,
forgive me my elision.

No Entry

Walking in the brightness and new cold
of a December morning, toward the stream
that marked the line between my neighbor's land
and mine, I heard its bubbling rush and gurgle
dimmed as though more distant. I approached
the water's edge and saw that overnight
a plunging snap with its sharp, sudden air
had candied over all the moving surface,
though the water surged along beneath.

No new-formed access was afforded there.
The stream was still too wide to jump; much as
the morning light leapt brilliantly from off
the skim, the ice could bear no greater weight.
The waters bumped and scrabbled underneath
as though in desperate search of open air.

So I was forced to walk in parallel
along a line that led us, I suppose,
to some unseen and distant sea, reflecting
that with another few nights like the last,
the stream would sink into a sleep, its racing
heart chilled down to stillness absolute –
left with nothing but a dream of freedom,
while I could cross at any point I wished.

One Goes to Zero

New Year's Eve 2019

One went to zero when she left
so was I of myself bereft.

Since nothing counted, nothing said
could raise a number from the dead.

Nor could my voice retain the power
to summon aught at any hour.

But changes of the turning year
can make a number reappear,

and zero will be seen again
when nine and one add up to ten.

The number inches on, unknown
until it's ready to be shown.

I'll see what may be rebegun,
the moment zero goes to one.

Only the Dead Are Perfect

June 26, 2019

I celebrate the day when, dazzled by
this bright, imperfect world, I first drew breath.
But every year, because it's unannounced,
unnoticed goes the day that marks my death.

So what if the day is hidden from me?
I know for certain that it will arrive.
And once a year I tread the calendar,
scuffing up a date I won't survive.

It could be any one, today included,
so why slight any secret future date
by failing to acknowledge what may be?
And since tomorrow may be named by Fate

the one in which I'll draw my final breath,
I'll keep in mind the possibility
and stay, till I'm perfected into nothing,
imperfect to the best of my ability.

Other Waters of March

An easy breeze has broken winter's back,
and sunlight stands up straighter on the snow.
whose softening awakes the almanac.
Melt water lisps its trickling undertow.

With each day in the forties through the week,
the last storm's cover can't help giving way;
What would it say, the snow, if only it could speak?
"I've hidden everything, but I can't stay.

The day is coming when the secrets kept –
all of them, both rare and ordinary,
so long forgotten by you as they slept,
will lie exposed again, open to query.

New bloom and festering: you must expect them.
Each to its fate, now that I can't protect them."

Paeanster to Punster

*for Christopher Ricks, on reading
his* Allusions to the Poets

Subtlest of punsters, he
provides convincing warranty
of trouble taken's worth
(I am not one who finds the pun
unsubtle from its birth).

Palimpsest

a manuscript on which the original writing has been effaced to make room for later writing but of which traces remain.

Music of the Florentine *Trecento* —
late fourteenth century polyphony
scored for voices, fiddle, lute, recorders,
and a clavisimbalum, the pieces
first written in the hand of the composer,
but lost thereafter for five hundred years,
the texts and the notation carefully
scraped off, to save the precious parchment for
a ledger to record church properties.

Its secrets slept in the illegible,
well lost, until the new millennium
brought forth multi-spectral imaging.
Its incantation spoke in scans and filters,
woke the seeming dead, commanded it
regain the page and take its place again
in time. I press a button, and the sound
leaps at me, shaped by specialists who take
their cues from newly printed manuscripts,
to body out the notes and give them life.

And as I listen to the plaintive call
of age old tribute to forgotten love,
I wonder if my own millennium
will ever turn, and if I'll get the means
by magic old or new to summon back
what I, the careful scribe, relentlessly

effaced from skin of memory – the song
I wrote in heart's ink copiously, when life
provided melody and rhythm, once,
before I scratched it out and overwrote it
with the blank numbers of the daily ledger.

Parra Makes a Point

after a poetry reading, Brown University, 1968

We three stood in close proximity,
the Chilean poet, and the North
American who did not trust in stories
but wrote books which resembled them somewhat,
and me, a student bent on understanding,

trying to make sense of the poet's words
when he had told us "everything that's made
by human hands has a reality
that's changed and different." Nasal in his vowels,
and creased of brow, the novelist protested:

"Ehhh, Nicanor, but I don't understaaand..."
His body, hunching forward, twisted slightly:
his struggle with the concept caused him pain.
"Like sausages," I said, and Nicanor
grinned in relief. "Yes, sausages, exactly."

Playing the Solo

To start, you have to choose a note to play.
The first question is not which one, but when,
(the chord you play it over helps you choose)
and then how long to hold it, and what shape

to give it, straight or bent or with vibrato.
Where do you go next? Jump up or down,
and by how much, or play the first again,
and right away, or do you leave a space?

The chord you play it over helps you choose,
but time is moving, and the chord may change,
and so you have to listen to the band,
and in the meantime listen to yourself.

This exercise of putting notes together
may make you think of others that you've heard,
so you may go that way awhile, and play
something familiar you can execute.

Or you may let it pass, and pick a note
that sends you in a different direction,
and play things that you never have before.
At the same time this is happening

you're not thinking at all, exactly, only
playing and reacting, listening
inside your head and outside all at once,
your mind a blank, and feeling your way through.

And feeling the emotion of the moment,
and singing it or dancing it, your sound
and steps made out of notes and silence.
But first you find your way to feel the time.

Because after you know the chords and scales,
you understand the possibilities,
and what at any moment is implied.
Strive to be always open to the moment.

Most players play around with chords and scales
and fill the air with notes, and sound the same.
Only a few can play around with time.
And every one who does is different.

Riders on the Climb

These days I don't go on the rollercoaster;
instead, I watch it from a hill nearby.
I care about the welfare of the riders,
since there but for the grace of God go I.

Not long ago I was myself a rider,
careful to drop the bar and hold on tight.
The clacking cars, the slowing on the climb,
imagination blooming into fright.

The general shrieks sheared off into the air
then, plunging of the innards like a stone,
the grip that mustn't slip felt through the knuckles,
your neighbor's knees plastered against your own.

Then all's a blur until a curve appears,
enough to get your bearings for the climb,
and it begins again. You steal a breath,
reset your grip, replant your feet, incline

your chin beneath your shoulders, and you're gone
beyond again, your screams torn from your chest
reminding you you aren't in control:
here is a moment different from the rest.

I sit out on a hill and watch it all,
a gently rolling slope beneath my feet.
Those distant riders on the climb are no
more helpless to what happens next than me.

Running Downhill

June 26, 2017

Careful, I place my foot down on the slope,
its carpet of dry needles, spruce and pine,
scumbled to tan by slanting light. The hope
is to trace out a path on the incline

where there is none, without a slip or fall.
Each footstep asks a question; settles in
to seeming answers, staying wary. All
can change upon the shifting of a pin.

The trees are sparse enough here to declare
a way ahead, and down too far to see
an outcome, but the roots and rock tips, bare
threats, are tripping opportunity

and promise ruin. Now the earth tilts more
with every step, and I lean back, as though
to cling to places where I've been before
instead of heading where I'm bound to go.

And the pins give, now I'm running down,
a sudden falling that's a kind of flying.
No place to put my foot, just push and ground
and rushing air; the present thought of dying

floods, huge in my sight. Ahead, a clearing
opens. In the settling light of day
beyond the trees, still somehow green, appearing,
the bright field where we children used to play.

Solstice Song

June 21, 2019

No, the days will not keep getting longer;
a curb's enforced that they may not exceed.
And there's a tide in the affairs of men
that won't keep coming in; it will recede.

The change, at first barely perceptible,
inexorable though it go unseen,
is brought about by labor in the heavens.
That day will come whose shortness makes it seem

the world will surely end in darkness, yet
that too will prove a too-hasty conclusion.
So minutes in this nightmare skitter by
and scatter our attention; the illusion

is it must be going on forever,
and everything is only getting worse.
Make a sacrifice if you're afraid,
but all that's really needed to reverse

the currents in the madness of the crowd
is pull the rope that Nature's pulling on:
what finally becomes too much will change
into a lesser thing, and with each dawn

its fury will be by a little spent.
And those who put their faith in argument
will wear themselves out trying to make sense,
while unseen forces make the difference.

Some Words

Some words are born to be misunderstood:
what's said to those who find the truth unwelcome,
however much it means to do them good;
what's put clearly enough, but lost on one

who isn't ready yet to understand,
but afterwards will realize too late
another way he could have played the hand
whose outcome has already sealed his fate;

those which intend a message so complex
a simple way to say it won't suffice,
whose meaning wriggles through the coarser nets
of language, and escapes its artifice.

Some words catch only by approximation;
the subtler truths elude our explanation.

Something Has Happened

I arrive to see the circles spread
across the quiet surface of the lake,

too late to see what's happened at the center
they flee from, even as they point a line

back to their start. But what set them in motion
is gone, already settled to the bottom.

Something Simple but Hard to Do

Listen to the whispers of your body.
If you don't, your body waits, then shouts.
Attend at once to what the whispers tell you;
if you hear the shout, it is too late.

Speaking Parts

The tapping drew me down into the basement,
its blunt insistence carefully controlled.
His cuffs rolled up, my Nannu sat, peered down
into the light that spilled across his workbench.

He was resoling; on the cast iron last
that makes me think of Giacometti now,
but then was just a duckbill upside down,
a dull brown boot was being tended to.

He tapped his funny nails in place; not one
was regular, each had a different shape.
He'd salvaged them from even older shoes.
When he was done, he lifted off the boot,

and taking up his hawk-nosed lino knife,
he trimmed the edges of the leather sole,
blade to his broad thumb, like he was cutting
hunks of bread, a fresh loaf in his hand.

He looked over his work, and with a bend
he shifted his position on the stool,
and it called out to me in groans and wrenching
of the wood where sturdy parts were joined.

The sounds reminded me of *Captain Blood*
below decks, when the ship pitched in the wind
or ran before it, offering reprieve
to oarsmen from the lash, however brief.

The theme those yelps and moans evoked was Journey.
My Nannu's shoes and boots, restored, afforded
him continuation, and the stool
itself has traveled through an age, to me.

Beginning life a hundred years ago
as kitchen chair, it had its back cut off
flush with the seat somewhere along the line.
When they broke up that house, my parents took it.

When I broke up my parents' house, I kept it,
since one could sit as easily from any
angle of approach. That's why it came
to rest at last in front of my piano.

And when I did my kind of traveling,
it gave me a support for voyages
into the depths that wait beneath the keys.
I'd find out what was mine, and bring it up,

its squeaks and wrenches my accompaniment.
Until one day it wobbled as it groaned.
I felt then, with his cobbling and my sounding,
how much our movements loosened up its screws.

So, taking on his role as a repairman,
I set a straight line driver blade with care
into those slots, left undisturbed for years,
and turn and tighten, hoping not to strip

the old screw heads, each cut a little different.
A final turn provokes a rising raunch
that signifies the wood is tight again.
its speaking parts restored, for now, to silence.

Splitting the Pod

As though I were a new pod of the milkweed,
split open by an eager child, exposed
to whim and wind and changing light of day,
my edges weep and sticky up the fingers
of the world, whose wish to wash itself
clean of me will have to wait. I dry
in open air, my seedlings lined up, dark
and slicked down, brooding in a fuselage
which will not keep, but can't remain itself
and fly. In time the downy tufts will soften,
fluff up and assume their natural form,
to parachute along the moving breeze,
and drift to altogether somewhere else.

The Art of Time

Often plentiful, sometimes in short
supply, time's our most natural resource.

It deals fairly with us, giving back
according to the way we give to it.

How we handle it determines whether
later we'll feel cheated of our lives,

or that the years have given us good value.
We can fill our time or empty it.

Full time is looked back on with satisfaction;
empty time is looked on in dismay.

Give all to a task, and time is filled,
although it passes imperceptibly;

absorbed with something other than ourselves,
we look up with surprise to see it gone.

But our investment in the moment lets
the years accumulate their store of ripeness.

Each day we grind to get it over with
is tossed aside, despised as valueless;

we think our life won't start until it's done,
so we withhold ourselves from what we do.

Such time heaps up, a pile of empty years
which leave us nothing, then are swept away.

The emptiest of empty days is wasted
in focusing on passing time itself,

each hour an enemy to be detained
for questioning, the battle in the distance.

The art of time is mastered only by
the daily practice of a lover's habit:

give all to time, and be repaid in full;
withhold yourself, and lose all in the bargain.

The Bells of Paradise

I saw a man who walked alone
Without a friend, without a home.
I asked him how it came to be
That no one spoke to him but me.

"My story is a cheerless one
Of a foolish and ungrateful son;
Though born of loving parents, I
Soon chose their guidance to defy.

Against their pleas I turned my back,
And set myself on a twisted track.
Rejecting them with pride and scorn,
I left the home where I'd been born.

With hardened heart I walked away
And grew more distant every day.
And as each morning came around
A cold, indifferent world I found.

I found no peace, I felt no worth;
I stood abandoned on the earth.
And finally I came to see
The author of it all was me.

To those I'd met, mile after mile,
I'd offered nothing – not a smile.
I'd lent no one a helping hand
Nor been a friend to any man.

Like sunlight flooding into shade
I saw the darkness I had made.
A devil's bargain I had kept
And carried Hell with every step.

I saw too what I had to do –
Begin to learn what others knew:
To use my long-neglected heart,
Go back to where I'd had my start.

With eager step I traced once more
The road that led back to my door.
What kept me going through the miles
My Father's voice, my Mother's smile.

I reached the town at close of day,
And walked again familiar ways.
At last the house came into sight,
And from within there shone a light.

So I strode up and rang the bell,
So much to ask, so much to tell.
A man came out unknown to me
And he said 'Yes, who may you be?'

I told my tale of long ago.
He shook his head, said 'I don't know –
This may have been your home before;
It's mine now – not yours anymore.'

I walked down to the burying ground
And searched the stones until I found

The ones that bore two names like mine
And chiseled dates of recent time.

The darkness started closing fast,
The words came tumbling out at last.
They glistened in the wintry air
But no one else could hear them there.

And this is why I walk alone
Without a friend, without a home.
It makes no difference where I go –
There's no place for me anymore."

He hung his head, he dimmed his eyes;
We heard the Bells of Paradise.
To him they sounded hopelessly
Beyond the reach of such as he,

Across a gulf of time and pain
That he could never walk again.
And so for him they tolled no more,
Nor led him on to Heaven's door.

We stood together on that ground;
To me they made a different sound.
They closer came, so I could hear,
And whispered closely in my ear:

"Be in the World, but see it true –
Let Heaven enter into you."
The opened gate within me lay.
I entered in that very day.

The Biblical Span: On Turning Seventy

June 26, 2018

The Psalmist gives us seventy, or more;
provided, that is, that our strength endure.

But I have had friends pass off from the scene
so many years too early, and have seen

my own strength ebb and flow away to next
to nothing overnight, and been perplexed

to find myself as weak as any child.
And so, no promises. I'm reconciled

to living out the letter of the lease
of Nature; from this day the terms may cease

at any moment to apply, and I
be thrust out of my dwelling, left to lie

all open to the elements. Evicted
despite my claim to further life predicted.

So now from month to month must be my measure:
the tenant stays on at the landlord's pleasure.

The Brave

Ruined and genteel at ninety-one,
he sketched the quiet of the room we shared
with drawn out husking from his phlegm-drenched lungs
throughout the night. Sometime midway he dared

to leave his bed to make it to the bathroom.
Unsteady, he went down at the threshold
in a heap, and shocked his forehead on
ceramic tile, his bright blood warm on cold.

Back in bed in daylight, he would talk
of how a man from Hospice said "Why go
back to the hospital? It wouldn't matter."
But he went. He wanted to explain.

"My ex-wife, we've been estranged for years.
We live apart, we don't speak any more.
But she relies on me for everything.
My every-other check goes to her door.

It's not enough for two. One day I eat,
the next she does. I made a promise, so
that's my responsibility to her.
I won't decide that it's my time to go."

The City Dweller Copes with Quarantine

You haven't lifted up your eyes to see
the spring in years. If pressed, you'd say you didn't
have the time, while jumping through the hoops
of making it to work, or getting caught
in traffic while the errands multiply.

So every year on branches overhead
the buds have crowned unnoticed on the stems,
and underneath your nose the blades of green
have cut their way through last fall's sodden leaves
to blaze a trail for this year's daffodils.

Indifferent to your inattention, Nature
goes about her business. Now, for once,
you're at a standstill. Be at last a witness
to the season. Let yourself be changed.
You too belong to reawakening.

The Dark Preserve

Car lights are flashing, we're all moving slow
down the side streets to the burying ground.
And you, my old friend, here we go
I follow you to where they'll put you down.

This field we pass is where we used to play
when we were kids, with no grown-up in sight,
and stay out till we couldn't see for day.
We hated to admit when it was night.

I hate the way the night's come on for you.
I thought there'd be a chance to play some more.
Now here's a thing I'm asking you to do
since you're the one who's going on before.

Tell the girl, you know the one I mean,
I'm sorry that I never understood.
She loved me in a way I'd never seen,
my love for her could never be as good.

I drove her to your arms, I see it clear,
and you turned out a better man than I.
What you gave her I never could come near,
It isn't fair that you both had to die.

So when you finally reach the Dark Preserve
and take your promised place, I hope you two
can give me what I wish that I deserved –
make me a place beside the two of you.

The Dead Are Otherwise Engaged

It may be that the dead keep to themselves,
having so much in common with each other,
and never lift their heads to look at us
at all, who are so little like them. They
can wait. We will be like them soon enough.

The Deadliest Are Not Like You and Me

Safe within my kitchen, I
regard the hawk with watchful eye.
His back is turned; in winter tree
I see him clear, he sees not me.

He moves his head; I hold my breath.
He peers, proposing certain death
below, on land. Against the sky
it's he that's brooding; or do I?

The Fearless

1.

In the midst of feasting the bright torches
guttered as the Great Hall doors were opened.
The room fell silent as a messenger
approached, for only the most urgent words
were permitted to disturb the Queen

at table. With his hair in disarray,
and road dust clotting at his neck and wrists,
he had been riding hard. A haste looked out
from his gaunt features, and the torchlight gleaming
in his eyes showed all an image of

a conflagration past, or soon to come.
He knelt before the Queen, reluctant to
speak up directly, looking round for one
to function as his intermediary,
as though his message needed softening.

But with her customary forthrightness
the Queen asked him to rise. "What are your tidings,
Sir? Be bold, and do not spare my feelings."
Not alone for this was she called Freda
the Fearless, for she'd proven herself in many

feats of arms in defense of the realm.
The King her husband had been killed in battle
ten years before. While he was in the field
she'd been delivered of their child, a daughter,

who also died that very day. Then, taking

up her partner's sword, she'd led the armies
in his place, and drove the foe out of
the realm time and again, when they encroached.
And so, clear-eyed, she heard all messages
of joy or woe with equanimity.

Thus encouraged by his Queen, the fellow
spoke out in a voice that all could hear:
"I man the outpost easternmost, along
the desert lands which separate us from
our warlike neighbors. In the drier years

that parched expanse forbids their crossing over
to trouble us, as they have often done.
This year we've had the rains, and looking east
I've seen dust clouds at morning mounting up.
Putting my ear against the drier ground,

I heard the treading hooves of a great host
massing near the borderland beyond.
I came at once to make this known to you."
The Queen looked down at him and smiled. "I thank
you, sir, for all your pains. Come, give him food

and drink, and make a place here at our table,
for he has proved himself a worthy subject
and deserves no less. And while his news
requires attention, let's not have it mar
good company, and interrupt our dinner.

Our neighbors stir themselves from time to time,

thinking they can enjoy all that we have,
but we will meet them as we have before."
A cheer went up throughout the hall, so calming
were her words, and all took heart to hear them.

Yet in her heart, behind her words, the Queen
was troubled. She had paid a price each time
she'd driven out the foe in seasons past.
Unseen beneath the metal of her armor
she carried scars of seventeen great wounds

she'd got in clash of armies, sword in hand.
And, deeper in her heart, unhealed, she felt
her blood still dripping for her man and child.
Yet all these were secret; and the people
cheered her fearlessness, and celebrated

the wild locks of her hair, bewildering,
which in the wind had shaken loose in battle
and left the foe transfixed and masterless,
a beacon leading on to victories
which ushered in a stretch of peaceful years.

2.

In the cool and shade of the grape arbor
the morning sunlight filtered through the leaves
and threw bright patches on the two sunk deep
in conversation: Osmun, stooped and old,
but in possession of the mysteries

of which few were aware, the master vintner;

and Sighi, grandson in his line, who was
apprenticed to him, carefully selected
to be the one to carry on tradition.
Osmun had been bringing him along

much as he did the living vines he tended.
In slowness, as the summer heat descended,
he was content to let both grapes and boy
grow to the sweetness that the harvesting
demanded. It was only on this day,

and only that the Queen called him away,
that he was compelled to let the lad
work on alone, without his guiding hand.
"So go ahead and make a sample must,"
he said, "choosing those grapes which ripened first.

A small batch will do. Take care to keep
it covered. Crush it thoroughly by hand.
Take out most, but not all, stems and seeds,
then add the Essence I keep underground.
That's the source of the Elixir's power,

and key to keeping its consistency.
Keep your batch both dark and cool, and don't
disturb it. I'll be back before it's ready.
In the meantime go ahead and start
the harvest. Do as much as time permits;

when I return we'll work again together."
Eager to please, excited to be trusted
in calling down the power of Elixir,
Sighi promised: all would be accomplished,

according to his master's strict instructions.

Preparing then for travel, the old man
gathered what he needed to appear
before the Queen, and set out on his way
with morning sunlight smiling on his leaving.
Sighi began his chance to prove himself.

Outside the arbor, and beyond the vast
expanse of vines, whose grapes were hanging heavy,
he could have seen the clouds of thickened dust
mount up skyward to the east. He could,
that is, if he were not so occupied.

3.

When Osmun was presented to the Queen,
she asked that her attendants leave the room.
"Come closer, Sir," she said, "to me you are
a name from long ago, though we have never
met. When I was just a girl, my father,

ill with the malady that claimed his life,
attempted to prepare me for the throne.
When he was near his end, he added one
more word of advice: if there should come
a day I was in need of what no one

could give, I should seek out the humble tender
of the vines along the eastern lands,
one Osmun by name, and he would have
the answer that I sought. More than a vintner,

he is a sage who safeguards mysteries."

Seeing the care which weighed down on her brow,
Osmun, stooped with age, bowed down still lower.
"I knew your father and his father too,
and on occasion they both called on me
for help. Since you ascended to the throne,

not once have I been summoned to your presence.
The people daily celebrate your rule;
the realm survives and prospers at your tending.
Relying on yourself has made us great!
What could cause you now to doubt yourself?"

"Nothing escapes your eyes! For doubt it is,
which I must not reveal to any others,
without imperiling our readiness.
Our neighbors once more threaten at our borders;
this time we may not beat them back again.

Belief in my invincibility
is strong among the people; they rely
on it to cheer them when the crises come.
So I may not betray a weakness felt,
but neither may I banish what I feel.

Each time past I've led us into battle,
I believed I could not be defeated.
But every victory has brought its wounds,
and every wound has left its scars. And other
wounds, from other times, still seep, unhealed.

I am not what I was, nor ever can

I be again. To think that I may fail
is all that it would take to make it so,
and open up a pathway for the ruin
of all I am, and all I would defend.

Your grey head has weathered many winters,
and so I am at ease to tell you this,
although it is my shame thus to confess
how far I feel from what I need to be.
But have you ever heard such foolishness?"

The old man straightened up and pursed his lips.
His face creased in a smile. "You waited till
you really needed me!" he said. "And that
was right. You'd found your way all on your own,
but now you doubt yourself. So here I am.

This is no foolishness. This is the change
that's brought about by time and human nature.
I can help you. I make an Elixir
which is a magnifier. It will grow
your strength a hundredfold at the first taste

and at the second any doubt will vanish.
It will allow you to become the best
version of yourself you can attain.
In past times it has served your family well
when your grandfather smote the foe in battle."

"I take heart from your words. The current threat
is dire, and on the present point of action.
Now is the time I must be at my best.
When may I taste the potent draught of which

you speak? Soon I'll be needed in the field."

"I have some ready, and will bring it to you,"
Osmun said. The far door to the chamber
opened then; a servant, apprehension
showing on his face, approached the throne
and begged indulgence for the interruption.

But there was news that could not wait. The vineyards
to the east had been surprised, the vines
first stripped, then torched. The winemaking equipment
had been taken, and the building razed
that housed it, leaving only ash and cinders.

The old man's brow was knit; his darkened eyes
looked far beyond the room. He drew a breath,
sharp and slow. "And what of my grandson?"
"No one was found, alive or dead," the servant
said. "Then he's a prisoner," Osmun said.

"Between what he knows and what they possess,
the danger is dramatically increased.
They'll find how to prepare their own Elixir,
give it to their troops, and turn its power
loose on us. They surely would prevail."

The Queen looked at him closely as he spoke.
She felt her life had changed since they had met,
and what had been a private doubt had sprouted
to a threat that cast a shadow on the realm
itself – and she resolved that she would face it.

"What can be done?" she said. Osmun thought long.

"Even if they learn the secret craft,
it will take time. My grandson may not tell them
everything; he's inexperienced.
This was to be his first experiment."

"And is your grandson brave?" the Queen replied
quietly, and thought of what it took.
"He is still a boy. If he's alive,
they'll test him as he's never been before.
The best that he could do is buy us time."

"But you are Master Vintner," said the Queen,
"could you somehow produce Elixir quicker,
let me take it, and ride out against
the foe before they have the time to make it?
If you could manage that, I like my chances."

"First, it's dangerous to try to rush
the process. Then we face a greater problem:
the right ingredients must be at hand.
It's possible to substitute the grapes,
but no one makes Elixir without Essence.

It provides the spark which sets the must aflame
and lets it loose to spur the transformation.
Mine has come down to me through generations;
I've kept it carefully, under the earth.
If it's been stolen, I am powerless."

"Can I get more? Where is it to be found?"
Freda exclaimed, her spirit leaping up.
"No one has gone there in my memory,
that of my master, or of his before him.

I've heard dim legends countlessly retold

among the masters, that its source resides
beyond the darkness, in the Western Lands."
"Then I must go at once, and you must tell
me all you know to guide me on the way."
"I know only so much; it may not be enough.

The way's beset with trials, formidable;
and you admit to harboring a doubt."
"If I am to lead, the task is mine.
I'd rather hazard my own life alone
than risk an army fighting at my side."

4.

As she spoke, she signaled to the sage
to hold his ground and not to speak. She padded
almost silently across the room, to where
a cabinet was standing near the wall.
She spoke up quietly then, to its tall door.

"Come out," she said with no tone of reproach,
not as command but gentle invitation.
"Don't be afraid, no harm will come to you.
I make this solemn promise as your Queen.
Come, let us learn why you have hidden here."

From out of the cabinet there stepped
a girl, as slender as a lath, in servant's
grey garb. Her skin and hair were variegated
in color, like the cousin whites and yellows

of new corn, and her pale eyes opened wider

and leapt about the splendors of the room
like sudden grasshoppers in summer heat.
She marvelled at the presence of the Queen,
who smiled at her as though to make her welcome.
"What is your name, my dear?" the Queen asked calmly.

"And why have you been hiding? Are you here
to do me harm?"
                "Oh no, nothing like that,"
the girl said, puzzled. "I was curious.
My name is Elle. I work down in the kitchen,
and every day the servants speak of you."

"I hope they say good things."
                "Oh, but they do!
They all say we are lucky you are Queen,
that only you can unify the realm,
and I could never find a better model.
That you are all I could aspire to be."

The Queen laughed quietly and shook her head.
"You are a daring and ambitious girl!
But what is it that you want to be?"
"I want to be the best at everything,"
Elle said after a moment's thought. "My best,

I mean. But I don't know yet what that is.
I've seen the best the Royal Cook can do,
but everyone says you do easily
what no one else throughout the realm can do.
I thought it best to find out for myself."

Amused, the Queen delighted in her candor.
"But surely you must have another model.
A parent, whom you could see every day?"
"I have no parents," Elle said evenly.
"I was a foundling left outside the palace.

An older woman took me in and let
me stay with her. She was a pastry chef,
and brought me to the kitchen where she worked.
I helped her all I could when I got big
enough. But she fell ill and died last winter."

"And all this time you've worked down in the kitchen?
How do the servants treat you?"
                                                "Most are kind,
except when they're so tired they can't stand up.
Then some of them think I'm just in the way,
and when that happens, they won't let me help them."

"Adults can be like that. I'm sorry you
were abandoned, and thrown in with them
so soon, and made to work. And now you're all
alone again, with no protector near."
The Queen paused, thinking of her own lost child.

"I didn't mind – there is so much to learn!
And my Aunt Raina always loved me well.
As for the rest, I live under your rule:
I am your subject, you are my protector.
You're never far away. What should I fear?"

The Queen was touched by this display of trust,
and shamed to think she harbored doubt within,

which she must act in spite of, and conceal.
"Truly," she marvelled, "those who call me Fearless
should lift that name and put it on your brow.

How old are you?"
                      "Eleven, as we guess."
"I would have had a daughter just that age,
if she had lived till now. I would enjoy
having a chance to help you grow. But now,
I haven't time to give you what you need."

"I know," Elle said, "I listened through the door.
You must go to the Western Lands. It's said
that darkness covers all there, and this man
spoke clearly of the many difficulties,
but you said you would go. You are the Fearless."

A smile broke slowly over Freda's face.
"I wish I was as sure of that as you!
I've always been before; it's carried me.
But now I have a doubt, and I'm confused
When the trials come, how will I act?"

"Then take me with you, for I have no doubt.
You'll see reflected in my eyes the Queen
you wish to be, for I can't see you otherwise."
"But I would worry that you'd come to harm."
"You'd never let that happen," said the girl.

Then Osmun, who had listened carefully,
spoke up. "It is no accident that at
this moment she has come into your life.
Where I must send you, there will come a time

where she will have a power you will not."

"A Queen should have a servant," Elle continued,
"I'll be both squire and handmaiden to you,
and I have learned the many kitchen arts.
You'll eat well. And I will keep you merry –
many a song is sung near a warm oven."

"I suppose you'll take the place of all my subjects,
one for all – I've always drawn my strength
from them. And so now I'll draw from you,"
the Queen remarked, but only half believing
her own words could be true; she wished them so.

Immediately they began to plan
their journey; every hour's delay increased
the danger. Osmun told them all he knew
about the path to take, and what they might
encounter, though he knew each trip was different,

and those who sought the Essence had to face
what each one found to be most difficult.
The adversaries took a different shape,
and they could change the nature of their power,
the better to attack one's greatest weakness.

5

The Western Lands lay out beyond the border
of Freda's realm. To get there you went through
a territory sparsely settled. People
there still clung to living in the light,

though there was less of it. Enduring twilight

left the landscape undergrown and bled
of bright green; tubers flourished underground.
It was said beyond the border people lived
who took the darkness as a commonplace,
embracing it for what it gave instead.

At first, there were still places they could stay.
The Queen disguised herself as Elle's protector,
as though Elle was from nobility.
It was good to see the people treat
strangers with warmth, as Freda would have done.

Once they moved beyond the settlements,
Elle more than earned her right to make the trip.
She had a knack for finding fresh sweet water;
she was adept at sparking up a fire.
Her clay lamp held a flame in any wind.

While Freda was a long-accomplished huntress,
the game that she brought down, and would have been
content to roast, stick-spitted, in a fire
took on a host of added flavors after
Elle rubbed in fragrant herbs picked on their way.

So they were well maintained as they approached
the looming mountains in the West, their peaks
obscured in gathering darkness. Only one
dim road through the landscape led them to
the narrow mountain pass they must traverse.

As little as the dwindling light afforded,

they made their camp just as they reached the foothills,
resolving to continue after resting,
both feeling the uncertainty ahead.
From the start, they had conversed in earnest.

They spoke as though they'd always known each other,
and Freda found she could speak easily
about her own lost child, what she had missed,
the damage she still carried – words she'd never
uttered before about her deepest feelings.

Elle took all of it in easily,
as though its power to hurt could be ignored.
Pain seemed to pass on through her without stopping,
and Freda was astonished that this girl,
although abandoned, never was diminished.

6

The next day brought the trip's first trial by arms.
Climbing in the foothills, following
the narrow path that only one could walk,
they made their way in file, with Freda leading,
to a clearing just before the pass.

It was legendary for admitting all
to enter, but none to return. The dead
were welcome, but the way barred to those living
who hoped to travel in the Western Lands,
gain some dark secret, and retrace their steps.

It was said that nothing in the lands beyond

was what it seemed. No map could correspond
to that terrain, meant as it was for those
who had no future. Landmarks once encountered
would move before they could be found again.

While this was daunting, first they had to gain
entry to the lands themselves, and darkness
like a thick mist huddled round the rocky
climes they clambered up to by mid-day.
The cleft that marked the way was hard to see.

Near the entrance, on a lofty perch
which afforded him a better view,
a small man with a shepherd's crook surveyed them.
"Do you propose to enter?" he called out,
"And will you be content to stay thereafter?"

"We seek a substance only found within,"
Freda exclaimed, "and then we must return.
There is a crisis in the Central Land,
and what we seek can save us, but to do so
it must be brought back to the land of light.

"That may not be," the shepherd-like gatekeeper
called out. "I must forbid your passing over."
Freda smiled to see her adversary.
"Then we must come to blows," she said, "for I
am pledged to gain the necessary prize."

"To trade in deadly blows is dire enough,"
the shepherd said, "but I am loath to rain
them on a woman's head. Retire, I beg you.
I would gain no honor separating

you from your life in such a likely outcome."

"That is an issue strokes will have to settle,"
Freda said. "My sword makes no complaint
that it is hefted by a woman's hand,
and you would suffer no dishonor by
your matching me in combat, win or lose."

"Very well," the shepherd said, and struck his staff
against the stony ground. Upon the instant
the gathering darkness lifted, and revealed
a rich pavilion trimmed in purple. Weapons
of all kinds could be clearly seen within.

The shepherd had transformed as well, into
a knight, dark helmed, in mail and armor clad,
in stature swelled up almost twice as large,
and promising in strength commensurate.
His staff had turned into a glinting sword.

"I am Noath, keeper of the pass,"
his said, his voice now clangorous and deep,
"I may not let you through, who mean to set
foot in the Western Lands and then return
to your other lives. This is my pledge."

Freda told Elle to find a sheltered place
among the rocks, and stay there, safe until
the combat ended. Then she turned her gaze
toward her adversary. "May just cause
guide my hand," she cried, and joined in conflict.

In early going Noath pressed advantage;
though their skill was equal, he was stronger,
and Freda leapt aside as deadly blows
glanced off the rocks at the perimeter.
She was more nimble, but as she got tired

her speed began to slacken. Noath forced
the attack remorselessly, kept moving forward,
and Freda felt herself give way, until
she thought, Queen that she was, of the welfare
of those for whom she was the Champion.

For their sake, then, she felt herself refreshed.
Her strength and spirit waxed; she battled Noath
back to a standstill on the open ground
before the entrance. With a sudden rush,
Noath's blade swept down at Freda's helm.

Her hair flew up as she transposed her sword
between them, but the force of Noath's stroke
shattered her blade in half, and left her holding
a spiky fragment. Noath then brought his sword
up once again to make another blow.

Seeing his arms go up above his head,
Freda saw a tiny opening
in time. Leaping from her knees, she brought
her shattered sword point up against his throat
and held it there before he could respond.

"Now yield, Sir knight, or feel a jagged edge,"
she said. Noath put down his sword and bowed.
"Until this day I never have been bested,"

he said mildly. "You have earned your passage.
But do not think this is your final trial.

Unparalleled as your lone feat of arms
has proved, so will you need your skills again,
and others which were not tested today.
Here, take my sword. Good luck in your endeavor!
You have been a matchless adversary."

Then Elle came out from hiding, and they both
readied themselves to take the mountain pass.
The rock, as they came close, arranged itself
without a sound to make a corridor.
Noath, again a shepherd, waved farewell.

7

With sheer rock on both sides, there was
no chance to put foot wrong despite the gloom
that settled all around them. They could feel
their way ahead, and knew they climbed up toward
the shrouded mountain peaks. The air grew cold;
they kept close and talked together quietly.

For none had told them what they could expect
as they descended to the Western plain
beyond the mountains. There the path was not
discernable; it flattened out and might
have gone off in a multitude of ways.

Nothing to see, no light to see it by;
if not for Elle's clay lamp, which threw a bit

of light around them, just enough to guess
the way forward, they would have had to stop.
In time the pathway flattened underfoot.

No sooner had they gained that Western ground
but they became aware of others there:
they drifted up, wraith-like and indistinct,
each a shifting column made of shadows.
Although they shunned the light, they gathered close.

They seemed drawn to the living creatures come
to their vicinity, all unexpected.
They tried to speak; their voices overlapped,
hollow as reeds, and curiously small,
as though their words had traveled a great distance.

They targeted both travelers, and veered
up next to each, their voices flaring like
mosquitos by the ear, and every one
the bearer of an urgent message from
the past, once lived and ever since remembered.

"My wife," one murmured, flooding Freda with
deep words of love, long lost and now recovered,
recounting moments from their lifetime shared.
But names and places, days begun and ended –
all were wrong, even the tone of voice.

And so the joy that leapt to Freda's heart
flew out and left it empty. Then another
came up presently and whispered "Mother"
close by her ear, and once again she felt
a pang. But all unrecognizable

in every detail of the living world
was this one too, and every one that followed.
And Freda felt a distance from them all,
and felt herself alone, and realized
she'd drifted almost out of sight of Elle.

A dull glow from her lamp was still somewhere
ahead, and Freda moved to make it brighter,
surrounded as she was by misty creatures
drained of all but feelings and the chance
details of memory. The light was hard to see.

But Freda focused on it; though horizon
lacked a line to separate a sky,
and though there were no objects underfoot
but only flat terrain obscured in darkness,
she made her way toward her young companion.

Elle was herself beset by shades, which gathered
close around her, and she welcomed them,
her clear voice in a running conversation.
When Freda got to her the lamplight billowed
enough to hold them both; the wraiths fell back.

So they went on, the light giving direction
along the line it seemed to penetrate
the farthest. Freda felt the need to speak
to Elle, to make sense of their late encounter.
"I thought at first my husband came to me,

and after that my child. I was mistaken.
They didn't really know me, and we didn't
really share the lives that they remembered.

I couldn't listen, or be reunited
with them, since we'd never been together."

Elle tossed her head and smiled. "But all is changed
here – names and places, times begun or ended –
they mean nothing here. It's feelings that
remain, and feelings flow from one to all,
and all through one. I spoke with mothers who

had given up their children, fathers who
went missing, died in jail, or fell in battle.
Feeling the victim, helpless, in despair –
one mother's feelings are much like another's.
From these I've learned so much about my life!"

Freda began to see how Elle could lead
the way for both of them. For all her strength
and force of will, if left to her resources
this vague place, without an obstacle,
would have swallowed them without a fight.

8

They stepped side by side, the keening wisps
of voices dimming in their wake as they
continued over flat land, as the light
from Elle's lamp led them on. After a time,
they found their eyes adjusting to the dimness.

Elle covered up her lamp, and gradually
they felt the contours of a landscape open
out into some gently rolling hills,

still greyscale, drained of color, but with features
unique enough to mark locality.

A broken line sketched out where a horizon
ought to be, though shadows in the distance
flickered up and back with every step.
Still they could see and feel their way ahead,
and they could sense a final stopping place.

For Osmun had prepared them for this point
where they would grow accustomed to the dark
and come to be one with it, just enough
to let them move on through this nether world
as though they'd never been in any other.

And he had told them what to look for now
that distances again could be perceived
and time to reach a destination judged.
A door built in a hillside would appear,
a day away by foot, and they should camp

out of its line of sight, and make their plan
before they could be seen. For though the door
was always left unlocked, that was because
its near approach was guarded by a Beast,
pledged to challenge those who sought to pass.

It was resourceful, and of monstrous powers;
as one eye drooped in sleep so would the other
quickly open, ready and refreshed.
And it was said it understood a challenger,
assessed each threat, and recognized its weakness.

Shapeshifting then, it turned itself into
the perfect adversary to defeat
any opponent, tailoring its weapons
to neutralize those of a challenger
and strip him of his confidence and spirit.

And while it had been beaten once before,
in the time of Osmun's great-grandfather,
he didn't know how that had been accomplished.
A different champion won that ancient battle;
this one would be fought on other terms.
Freda tried to picture how to do it.
Surely this Beast would know about her doubt
and move to bring it out into the open;
then she would have a fight within herself
that held her back before she struck a blow.

If she could sneak up as the monster's eye
was falling off to sleep, behind that closed,
unseeing one, and time a deadly stroke
to lop its head just as the other opened –
but she would have one chance, never another.

She thought that Elle might be of use, distracting
the Beast as she crept up behind it, but
she thought again to keep her out of danger.
And so she didn't tell her of the plan
that night. They rested up before the battle.

9

The mornings in that land were even dimmer
than the evenings. They set out to take

a roundabout approach, to go unseen
behind the hillside and its guardian.
Freda cautioned Elle to stay in cover.

She relied on absolute surprise,
and nothing must disturb the drowsy Beast
once they were close enough. So Elle took up
a place concealed among the hills nearby,
from which she had a clear view of the entrance.

As Freda padded silently behind
the snorting Beast, whose labored breathing spoke
of need to close an eye in rest, and rushing
air from in and out its flaring nostrils
drowned out the careful steps of her approach.

Elle's eyes grew wide as Freda came up by
the hulking body of the Beast, her sword
arm raised in readiness behind the eye
as it seemed to flutter before settling,
the far side other eye about to open.

She brought her arm down like a sudden
flash of lightning brightening the sky;
beneath the fury of the blow, the head
should then have fallen. But instead, the blade
passed through the massive neck as though through air.

Freda recoiled, and felt a sudden coldness
through her limbs. She knew she couldn't
strike a greater blow, yet this had been
as nothing. All her doubt rose up; she shivered
at the prospect of tbe Beast's response.

The Beast, in fact, had hardly noticed it,
and idly scratched behind its head, as though
some nuisance itch needed attending to.
With that, its other eye clapped open, turned
in its socket, and discovered Freda.

But before it could address this creature
come to test its patience, it was moved
to hear a child's voice out in front of it,
singsong, a playground ditty, as she skipped
up to the Beast and stopped, arm's length away.

Freda was forgotten then, as Elle
called her own cadence and began to dance.
The Beast looked on in wonder at the child
who leapt in joy before it, reaching out
and offering to join with it in play.

Now it was Freda's eyes which widened at
the sight of the great Beast, cavorting with
a slender child, corn kernel white and yellow.
They kept it up until the Beast collapsed
into a heap, emitting sighs of pleasure.

Elle patted it upon its head, and strode
up to the door, cueing the Queen to follow.
It opened easily, and they went in.
What a crystal cave was cut into
that hillside! Dark without, but bright within,

as though they'd penetrated to the heart
of a great geode, redirecting light
in all directions, with an inner chamber

glowing up ahead, suffused in blue
and promising an unfamiliar warmth.

Once inside that chamber they were struck
by the enchantment of the place: a bubbling
spring provided a refreshing pool,
and floating on its surface, undisturbed,
a flower like an orchid bloomed in blue.

Elle went up and gently harvested
the silver dust which sparkled on its petals.
They cleaned off to a deeper hue;
even the luminescent grotto walls
inclined their tint to Lapis Lazuli.

As they retraced their steps and finally
emerged out of the hillside, passing by
the deeply sleeping Beast, lost in contentment,
Elle turned to Freda and apologized.
"I'm sorry that I had to disobey you."

Freda, still astonished by the girl,
said "I thought you had to be protected,
but it was I who needed help. You saved
both of our lives, and brought us to our goal.
What else could I do except to thank you!"

"But you are still my Queen. It's just that I
could see you would have trouble with the Beast,
and I knew the way to handle him.
He'd been a monster, even as a child;
a monster never has a chance to play."

Freda recalled the words that Osmun said
before they left, that she should take Elle with her
for there were places she could enter, where
even the Queen would find herself denied.
This child possessed a deeper understanding

which let her see beyond the world's disguises.
She had an innocence, unbroken by
abandonment, that let her act without
a flinching in advance from pain or failure:
she walked on earth, on air, on fire, on water.

10

Freda pondered long on their return.
This girl had showed her that an unscarred heart
possessed the power to transform the world.
If at one time that power had been hers,
the loss of it had joined the other losses

that had robbed her of her innocence,
and left her hardened to the direst outcomes.
She saw herself opposed, anticipating
the worst, the last hope of preventing it.
She was accustomed to self-sacrifice.

Her subjects saw her as a paragon,
with strength they lacked, without the fears they felt.
Although the role was insupportable
she'd played it for their sake, and for the sake
of those she'd loved whose places she had taken.

She'd paid the price of being just as human,
just as vulnerable to doubt, and kept
it to herself. Her fearlessness consisted
in fighting off her doubts before her battles,
and never letting on she was conflicted.

This was a wearing role to play, despite
her willingness. And now, with ease, this girl
upends her world of constant adversaries,
showing the seams of new realities,
to which by nature Freda had been blind.

And while possession of the Essence lent
them both a special grace which smoothed their way
and sped them home, she knew that waiting there
a battle would be joined; she couldn't know
if her kind of strength would be enough.

When they returned, her face, when seen abroad
among her people, brought them cheer again.
With war clouds threatening, they had misgivings,
though they supposed their Queen was occupied
with preparations carried on in secret.

11

And strictly speaking, that had been the truth:
while they were off to get the necessary
all powerful ingredient, the vintner
had been hard and hastily at work
to find the right grapes and prepare a must.

No moment could be spared; assuming that
their enemies had stolen crop and Essence,
and had taken someone who knew how
to make Elixir, they had a head start
giving them a dangerous advantage.

In the privacy of chambers, Elle presented
Osmun with the precious silver dust;
though he had known the child would play the crucial
role that led to their success, he hadn't seen
what she would do. He listened eagerly.

Wisdom of youth and age had worked together
to get them to this point; but now the hazards
palpably increased. "The Essence, yes,"
he said, and turned the tiny leather pouch
around to open it. "We have a chance.

But here's the problem – they've begun already.
Elixir must go through two transformations
before its power is developed fully,
and it has a chance to settle down.
It takes six months to finalize the process."

"But wouldn't that give us plenty of time,
and couldn't our Elixirs both be ready
almost together?" Freda asked, and brightened.
"It would, if only everyone were patient.
What if our enemies don't want to wait?

The must assumes its power in the first
transformation, though the liquor comes
out raw and unpredictable. It may

magnify one's strength; it may diminish.
It's purely chance – it's different every time.

If our neighbors to the East are so impatient
they won't wait out the fining of the brew,
they could elect to take their chances, drink
it while it's raw, and risk the consequences."
"How soon could they do that?"
       "Two or three weeks.

I'll start our own batch right away, but I
must warn you – grapes were hard to find. I have
enough to make a limited supply.
They carried off our crop, enough to give
to every warrior before a battle.

What it would do to them no one can say,
but they could choose to try it very soon."
Freda said, "Make what you can. I've faced
this situation more than once before.
I'll make the necessary preparations."

So with invasion hanging in the air,
Freda readied her defending army.
If it came to that she'd take the chance
and drink the raw Elixir Osmun made,
hoping it would help her in a battle.

To acknowledge Elle, she moved her up
to spacious quarters, closer to her own.
The kitchen staff were filled with wonder, seeing
a foundling waif, so often underfoot,
now treated more like Freda's own lost daughter.

And in the troubled weeks that followed, as
all eyes and ears were trained upon the border
for signs of an attack, both Queen and child
spent happy hours together, finding in
each other something both had been denied.

12

But soon that idyll had to end; the signs
of armies massing on the Eastern border
were unmistakable, and it was clear:
invasion now was imminent, a matter
of a day, or even less than that.

Freda camped her army out at night
on level ground outside the city gates,
in hopes of keeping those within the walls
out of harm's way. The battle, she could feel,
would come, perhaps as soon as in the morning.

Concealed within her tent, she met with Osmun,
her most trusted lieutenants, and with Elle,
for she had learned keeping her close was better.
When the danger of a situation
was at its greatest, Elle was powerful.

The Queen began by drinking the Elixir,
raw and cloudy, unpredictable.
"You'll feel more like yourself," the vintner said,
"at least at first your strength should grow. But after,
almost anything could happen. Watch

closely that your judgment's not affected,
for strength that carries out a bad decision
can only help you make a worse mistake.
It may be that the fight you have within you
proves harder than the one you have before you."

Thinking of her encounter with the Beast,
the Queen remembered how she'd needed help
with both those fights. She hoped this would be different.
Calling aside her officers, she said,
"Remember they always attack at dawn.

They'll come straight at us, with the sun behind them,
when the first light is flat against the ground.
For several minutes you'll be almost blinded;
they'll see you perfectly, you'll see a glare
and squint your eyes. Exactly then, they'll strike."

Her officers were murmuring assent
when Elle stole up and whispered in her ear.
At that the Queen issued another order;
the lieutenants promised to obey,
and quit the tent to fan out to their troops.

13

Freda's army rose before the dawn
and spent two hours preparing in the dark.
No one, not even they, could see what they
were doing. Just before the rising sun
had broken the horizon with its rays,

the opposing host raised up their swords
as high as they could reach, enough to catch
the first light on their waving blades. The mass
of moving flashes looked like fireflies
swarming in a band, and as the sun

split the distant line and shot across
the flat terrain that separated them,
they brought down their arms and spread apart;
the flood of sunlight blinding their advance,
they broke into a run at the defenders.

Now Freda and her army, standing close
together as they'd planned, put up their shields,
each tall and touching, gleaming like a mirror.
This was the task they'd carried out before
the dawn: a flawless surface, polished in the dark.

They fell back into a gentle curve, so that
the morning light was focused and reflected back
into the eyes of the advancing host.
At first it kept on coming; then, out on
the open plain, its ranks began to waver.

As though confusion settled over them,
the foe broke ranks and ran awry; and then,
to the astonishment of the defenders,
as Freda looked beyond the wall of shields,
they turned to rain their blows upon each other.

Wherever light reflected off a sword,
each man identified an enemy,

and raised his own to strike another blow.
Thus multiplied by fighting at close quarters,
the attackers took a deadly toll.

Without lifting an arm in their defense,
the army of the Queen observed its foe
reduce itself to a crazed mass of dead
and dying. By the time the sun had risen
fully, not one seemed to be alive.

Above the hacked and smoking heap of bodies,
the last groans of the slain had all subsided,
and silence settled on the place of battle.
But Osmun's eyes, old though they were, could vault
the distances to a familiar figure.

"Sighi, my boy!" he cried, and waved his arms.
Out beyond the battlefield, one lone
and standing figure waved back instantly.
He made his way around and through the fallen
until old man and boy were reunited.

Unharmed and in good spirits, Sighi smiled.
Osmun introduced him to the Queen.
"We're glad that you survived!" Freda exclaimed.,
"Can you explain what we've just witnessed? Did
you somehow find a way to make it happen?"

"It took some luck," Sighi began, and shook
some dust out of his curly hair. "They knew
what they were doing and exactly what
they wanted. After you had left," he nodded
to Osmun, "they came when I was alone.

I saw I couldn't stop them, so I went
along. I was well treated, so I knew
they needed me to show them what to do
to make Elixir. They had taken all
they needed, must and Essence and equipment.

They left nothing behind. I didn't think
you could make more. I thought I could adjust
the recipe enough to sour the batch –
by using too much Essence it could go
wrong in lots of ways. I made it clear

Elixir had to age for many months
before its power could be depended on.
Of course they couldn't wait. I didn't tell
them what could happen if they took it raw.
Their whole army drank it late last night."

"If we could have, we'd have done the same,"
Freda said thoughtfully. "We wouldn't wait,
knowing they wouldn't. We'd have met the same
Fate, fighting with ourselves. Perhaps like them,
not even one of us would have survived."

"It's as though a madness came upon them,"
Osmun said. "Their judgment went awry,
and anyone seen carrying a weapon
became an enemy. That's why, my boy,
you alone came through the fight untouched."

"Yes," Sighi replied, "I had no weapon."
Freda thought long after hearing him.

Together, these two children saved the realm,
and neither of them wielded sword or shield.
Their fearlessness was of a different sort.

She spoke out clearly to her followers:
"I too have drunk Elixir unrefined
The battle was resolved before my mind
misled me, but it may at any time.
Lock me up until the fit has passed.

Till then, this girl, this boy, and this old man –
without whom we would not be safe today –
using their judgment, will rule in my absence.
After my release, they'll be my closest
confidantes, wiser by far than me.

You call me fearless; that's no longer so,
if it ever was. My heart is scarred,
and only the unscarred are truly fearless.
Fearless or not, I've lived relying on
myself, and my own strength. That day is over.

Here are three who see what I can't see,
do what I can't do, and understand
what I've never thought of, never could.
I need their help. My world is limited,
while theirs is full of possibilities.

See that our adversaries are respected;
bring the fallen back across the border
so that their families may honor them.
Let them know we seek no further conflict.
Mind your new leaders well. Take me away."

The Queen was locked up in a room for two
days and nights. She spent them silently
and offered no resistance to her keepers.
She thanked them when at last she was released,
Back in her court, she met with her advisors.

They were curious about her time apart.
How had the raw Elixir shaken her?
What distorted visions overtook
her mind? Were there attackers everywhere
she looked? A sad expression crossed her face.

"I must confess to you," she said, "but it
must be our secret. I began to feel
a change come over me the instant that
I drank. Yes, well before I told you, in
the night we spent preparing for the battle.

I was seized with fear – we couldn't win
the coming fight. The troops were unprepared,
the officers all unreliable.
My first thought was to offer single combat,
hand to hand, their champion and me.

The armies would withdraw, accept the outcome.
But then my mind raced to their chosen hero;
I couldn't know his strengths, exploit his weaknesses.
There were so many ways that I could lose.
I saw the city sacked, the realm enslaved.

These visions all contended in my mind
at once, and as I stood transfixed before

my officers, you, child," she turned to Elle
and smiled, "came up and whispered in my ear
the tactic of the sun and polished shields.

I was repelled by what you said. I felt
the wish for combat rising in my throat.
This was a time for shedding blood,
and I had been anointed for the task.
Your words would have us win without a fight.

My life, you see, had trained me for this moment.
I'd won so many battles in the past
it felt wrong to rely on someone else.
I could see no other way to lead.
But then I looked at you. I trusted you.

So even though my mind was in revolt,
and every fiber of my body feared
relinquishing control over the moment,
I gave the order you had told me to.
I had all I could do to stand and watch.

When in the morning the invading army
fell savagely to butchering each other,
I knew the way they felt. I would have raised
my arm and struck out blindly at the shadows –
except that I held on to trusting you.

And when the day was settled, there came over
me the sweetest feeling of release,
as though a heavy mantle had been lifted.
I had shared the burden; we had won.
How freeing it is, not to be the hero!"

The Gift

for Chuck Goldberg on his turning 70

Born into this world where suffering
is spooned somewhere on everybody's plate,
he had a gift for feeling. All its forms,
not only joy and pain, but in between
as well, and not what came to him
alone, but what across our barriers
is felt by all of us. As though compassion,
which for some of us comes hard, for him
was right away as natural as breathing.

But the pain of others is a blade
without a handle; grasping it exacts
a cost that we can never finish paying;
they are so many, and their pain so great.
The wounds are open everywhere we look.
The danger is that we will feel so much,
we're paralyzed. It's only self-protection
to look away. And so we toughen up
our tender hearts, the better to move on.

But this is not the way he's used his gift.
No hardening of the heart; he softens it.
He has the empath's talent for connection.
He understands – the purpose of compassion
is to be moved to service. Here's a way
of living with the sorrows of the world.
So many wounds are deeper than your own,
devote yourself to meeting others' needs.
If you can't heal directly, help the healers.

When you commit to serve, you put your own
concerns aside, and like the servant in Isaiah,
you take the pain of others on yourself.
Confronted with a world of suffering,
instead of shrinking back, you open out.
And in that sharing, there's a saving grace:
for as we work to heal the wounds of others,
we feel our wounds begin to heal as well.
Is there a better way to use a gift?

The Magi Lose Their Way

Christmas Day, 2016

On our journey from the Eastern lands
the new star in the night sky kept us on
the path through many difficulties.
Out of compass from our constellations,
it made an easy guide, glowing and low
hovering above that distant place
where lay the infant king we'd heard about.

But on the way we passed a city ruined,
desolated utterly by war.
Not one stone there stood upon another;
no one could be found to tell us how
or why they'd met their fate, but smoke hung thick
above the rubble, troubling the sky,
as though the earth had somehow wrapped itself
in its own winding cloth. The crackling embers
in the wreckage made the only sound,
their faint, dull glow the only dying light.

The waste of that place made us pause, until
we saw the grounded sky bereft of stars
and realized we'd lost sight of our guide.
What heaven had provided, men on earth
had labored to obscure. Which was our way?
At first we were despondent, overwhelmed
to think that such fair promise could be lost.
Contagious in that place, the darkness dimmed
our faith itself, and it was tempting to
sit down, curse humankind, and brood on chaos.

But that would end our journey. Then the dark
itself, tasting of iron, gave us the answer:
the ash that clots our lungs and coats our tongues,
the grit that irritates our eyes, and sticks
between our teeth, this shroud that pins us down
to earth, is just another kind of cloud;
the stars we reckon by still burn beyond.
We are without original direction,
but any heading is away from death.

So we set out again despite confusion,
blinded by what men do in this world
but trusting if we stayed on any path,
however crooked man has made the maze,
we would regain our sight, reorient
ourselves, begin anew – and yet attain
what may be reached from any starting point:
the sacred ground of the nativity.

The Next Idea

I make a space for it, and it appears.
I feel it coming on, as though I'm filled
flush to the brim and then beyond. It spills
up, out into the light; its image clears.

It soon declares itself, and calls by name
what I must call it, and must let it be.
My mind is empty; I wait patiently
and watch it take its shape within the frame.

It often comes continuous, complete.
Sometimes I need to pause and clean the way,
but trusting as I do that it will say
all that it needs to when at last we meet.

Such visits have been going on for years.
I make a space for it, and it appears.

The Rise of a Sparrow

I shot three arrows quickly one two three,
and as the cliff edge near my feet stood high
beyond all measure, I sat down to wait,
not knowing when they'd hit or miss their targets,
barely showing on the plain below.

At first the multiple uncertainty
kept me from knowing any way to feel;
but then I saw a sparrow dip from left
to right, from close behind me to the brink,
veer down beyond my sight, then sudden up
out of the blank space, swooping into view
and disappearing back along the path
I'd taken. And it made me smile, forgetting,
for a moment, distances and outcomes.

The Substitute

During the Original Cast recording of the Harold Arlen – Truman Capote musical House of Flowers *in 1955, cast member Diahann Carroll, who was suffering from a cold, had trouble with one word near the end of her feature "I Never Has Seen Snow," and it had to be patched in by another singer.*

Her voice finely controlled, delectable,
Diahann Carroll made her mark throughout
the song, her ardor and sincerity
announced and held out to the audience.

So when she couldn't finish at the end
and just a word in the last phrase, one word
which would have snapped the taut thread of her spell
had to be redone by someone else,

who else to do the job but the composer?
A cantor's son from Buffalo, he started
as a singer, Hyman Arluck, changed
his name to Harold Arlen, and the rest

was film and theater history. He dusted
off his tenor, lean and bright, and trimmed
it, softened back to half-voice, all unguarded.
But nothing like the voice of Diahann Carroll.

And yet they got away with it. By that
point in the song the people were convinced:
they thought they knew what they were going to hear.
They listened to but didn't listen for.

However, once you know it's coming up
in the last phrase, you're shocked – it jumps out at you.
You don't see how you ever could have missed it.
Such is the power of a false belief.

The Sweetest Sound

An actor in a farce will prize the laugh –
the surest sign he's hit the mark. Sometimes
it rushes from the darkness like the turning
of a tap, full-throated gushing water.

Other times it trickles fitfully
as voices straggle. Either way you wait
until it's run its course, and time the beat
as it abates, to start your line again.

But it is always welcome. Better still,
the sweetest sound I ever heard onstage
came once in a silent house, the play
a tragedy, the scene intense, when as

the older brother, slighted and ignored,
I crossed in quiet triumph downstage left
to make my mother sign the fateful papers,
my purpose clearly reprehensible.

The audience, as though with one voice, hissed.

The Tree That Didn't Know It Was a Fruit Tree

The tree that didn't know it was a fruit tree
grew up in a grove of evergreens,
shy about the shaping of its leaves,
un-needle-like, and shocked to see them fall

in that first season, and to stand denuded,
open to the winter wind, surrounded
by pines and firs, secure and durable,
cloaked in close green, with silver underneath.

Flush in the spring, astonished by its budding,
the new growth answers with a brighter shade
the somber questions coloring its neighbors.
Then, taken unawares by blossoming,

and gaping at its petals, pink and white,
it keeps a secret in the mystery
of pollen, to be visited by bees
who find their way to it, unerringly,

to share that secret in a distant place.
It marvels as a different change ensues
from pollinated blossom into fruit,
which swells and ripens through to harvest time.

What is this crop that bumps against the carpet
of crackling brown, and settles down upon
the layered needles of the forest floor?
It doesn't understand the rot that follows,

the role that beauty plays, fruits ripening
into a sweetness; why they had to die
to make way for new life. Among its neighbors
alien, and ill-equipped to know

its mission while it thinks itself alone,
it stands, as animals approach and nibble
at its gifts, to leave the bitten cores
behind; ahead, the site of future orchards.

The Unforgivable

Something happened on her honeymoon:
The Unforgivable. A day or two,
a week at most, she showed up back at home,
never to speak of what she'd been put through.

Living again with parents and her sister,
with no thought of annulment or divorce,
she kept her husband's name until she died,
and bitterness and shame had run their course.

But not one day before. The way she spoke
his name in conversation gave a chill:
laced with contempt, familiarity,
and helpless hanging on the words that kill.

I was her cousin's son, born in what would
have been the time of her own children's birth.
And I was prized each Sunday after Mass
out of all proportion to my worth.

Fed the precious saved-up delicacies,
Torrone nut and nougat, hard to chew
but not to be declined, and sugar iced
egg cookies, chocolate mint pan candy too,

all too sweet by half. When I was older
it was anisette and fresh pizzelles,
still soft and bendable, warm from the iron.
Gifts lavished on me so as to compel

my sitting still for those two single sisters,
one knotted up by marriage all too brief,
the other four foot six and hunchbacked, thought
fit only for the convent. What relief

their substitute affections could provide them
I never knew, but they were always kind
despite all the demands of their devotion.
I kept The Unforgivable in mind.

What could have soured the new bride on her man
so thoroughly she never could let go,
yet never could accept? The mystery
was deep; even my mother didn't know.

When I was old enough, my father took
me to the barbershop. Amid the smell
of tonic and Vitalis, clipping hair,
men's talk, and quiet with his clientele

stood the man in question, plain and trim,
with black rimmed glasses and a patient air,
adjusting the position of a head,
applying gentle pressure here and there.

In short, he didn't fit the story line.
Unlikeliest of monsters, he was tame.
Which only brought me back to the dilemma
of what he'd done, for what he was to blame.

So here's the rub: was he a specimen
of vileness out of mind, so well concealed

he bore no single trace of evil nature
until in secret it could be revealed

behind the closed door of the bridal chamber?
Or was his sin common in man and wife,
grown monstrous in the eyes of one who'd led,
much to her grief, a far too sheltered life?

Might we judge she was too sensitive,
her hopes disgorged, too quick to run away
and settle for a life in opposition
to the absent one who'd come to stay?

We will never know the truth of this.
All principals are dead, all secrets kept.
What is The Unforgivable, to you?
What in and of itself can't you accept?

The Uses of Ignorance

If you can look into the seeds of time,
and say which grain will grow and which will not ...
                                    MacBeth I, iii

Today is spring; tomorrow will be winter.
The radar shows a snake-like front along
the coast from Hatteras on up to Maine,
and temperatures will plunge, with snow to follow.

Growing up almost a hundred years
ago, my father learned how not to trust
blue skies and sixty on a February
day here in New England, but he had
no way to tell what would be coming next.
Every lesson took him by surprise,
so he became resilient to fate.

I can see the future, serpentine,
arriving overnight, blind to intent.
Beyond the stocking up on milk and bread,
my inner weather would survive as well
without a forecast. Better not to know,
submitting to the hammer blows that shape us
until we are prepared for anything.
Don't anticipate, I say: be ready.

Through a Window

High summer. In my second floor apartment
the night is thick with unremitting heat;
I go to the front room to open windows
all the way, while hoping for a breath

of moving air. There's not the slightest stir.
Even the darkness lies against my skin
like a hot wet sheet I can't throw off.
Opposite from me, across the street,

light shoots out from a neighboring apartment,
but only I can see into the room,
its curtains drawn back as if in a play;
my view is level with the furniture.

There isn't much. A couch and coffee table
are all the newly moved in tenants have
so far, the walls are blank of decoration.
A stocky, balding man, beer can in hand,

in stirrup T shirt, shambles through the room
and settles on the cushions, carefully.
I freeze, although he likely couldn't see me
in the dark. And then, he isn't looking.

Instead he sips the beer and stares in profile,
straight ahead. Out from the depths beyond
the room, a girl, somewhere between too young
and far too young, emerges into view.

She's slender, in a slip. Her hair is long
and sways against her straps. She holds a blue
balloon, a full length broadly ribbed torpedo,
taller by a head, in close embrace.

And she waltzes it around, deliberate
and slow, as if held in a gentle trance,
and moving to a stately unheard music.
But the windows gape and night is still;

there is no music as he looks at her.
Around the room she moves in lazy circles,
absent eyes fixed on her dancing partner.
Unwilling to see more, I turn away.

To a Young Singer

Is it because you're young that when I hear
you sing I can't tell who's behind the words?
Your voice is blank and reedy, scrubbed of region,
and when you sing of life I don't believe
you've lived through the ordeals you sing about.

When I listen to a song, I need
to feel I know who's bringing it to me.
Like I'd listen to a tale of woe
across a table in a quiet bar
because I liked the guy, and knew

he couldn't help himself, he was so full
of what had happened he just had to tell it
or bust. I'd do that for a friend in need,
or anyone for whom I felt a kinship.
But hearing you, I don't know what you sound

like when you're meaning every word you say,
much less meaning every one for me.
Convince me – I'm the one who's listening,
after all, instead of having lunch.
I've paused my life so you can have your say.

Too Green

She left me for the man she was to marry
years later. Truth is I drove her away.
Her love for me had never been in question.
I read the notice of her death today.

We hadn't passed a word in forty years.
They'd moved to Florida, opened a stable
with a riding school. They taught dressage,
three day eventing – passions she was able

to build a life around, and with a man
who shared them. All were gifts I couldn't give.
I imagined she was better off.
But there had been a life for us to live

in love together in that distant time
when we were both deciding a direction:
five years out of our youth, discovering
the depth and quality of our connection.

And we were innocent of how we could
be changed, in ways we'd never known before,
when we'd awarded with the name of love
strong feeling. This was different, and more.

We found ourselves buoyed by each other's presence,
which seemed always immediate and here –
for suddenly we'd breathed each other in
and we were easy in the atmosphere.

So we renumbered days together, from
the first appearance of love's true expression.
Gradually we trusted in the future;
there seemed to be no end to the progression.

I joined a band that traveled every day.
And there were women listening every night,
dancing at our feet, and smiling up
to catch my eye. I knew it wasn't right.

But there was a lure in the unknown,
and a new unknown tomorrow night.
The thought made me somehow unsatisfied
with what I had, compared to what I might.

So when she asked if we could live together,
I held back, and used a lot of words
I didn't mean, to keep her on the string.
But what she wanted wasn't what she heard.

I wasn't honest; I was immature.
But knowing I would not be otherwise
for who knew how much time to come, I was
a coward to content myself with lies.

And then she told me she had taken up
with someone else, to shock me. I could feel
the chill that numbed me to her hidden plea.
And so I let us drift out of the real.

I learned years later how she must have felt
when I was finally ready for forever.

Another woman got to play my role
and show me why we couldn't be together.

Once on our road, we can't be anywhere
but where we are. If we could jump ahead
or go back a little, we could make
levels of readiness match up. Instead

despite our efforts and our will, we often
appear to be in step, but only for
a little while. Too green, my love was not
enough, although I wish it had been more.

So blame's beside the point; I couldn't have
been otherwise. But shame's still in the way,
and there's regret for what I threw aside.
I read the notice of her death today.

Trickling Up the Jug

When trickling up the water in the jug,
that point partway where you would swear the level
isn't rising is sure sign that you,
yourself, are the corruptor of your world,
by introduction of an expectation
which interrupts perception of the flow,
and which you're powerless to stop. The water
mounts up, innocent in spite of you.

Unanswered Prayers

*In love there is always one who kisses
and one who offers the cheek.*
                French proverb

Some friends will never be the first to call.
They know I'll get in touch eventually.
And I don't find it onerous at all
that making the first move is up to me.

Their silence doesn't indicate a lack
of interest; they are genuinely glad
to hear from me, and often answer back.
But when they don't, I'm neither hurt nor mad.

A prayer may go unanswered. Still, I find
some satisfaction putting into words
all that I need to say. And I remind
myself to trust that I've been heard.

Our bond is one not prematurely broken
because a word I long for goes unspoken.

Unofficial Love

The rain that washed out last night's game before
the fifth cancelled official recognition
of the feats performed – the three home runs,
the sparkling outfield play, the details of
the box score – just as if they never happened.

But I was witness to them, so I know
they were as real as any others you
could look up in the records of this game
which claims a privilege: time doesn't run
out, but only ends when play is done.

Like one college girlfriend, who pronounced
not only that our short-lived flame was dead,
but it had never really burned at all,
we feel a need to wash away the past
from time to time, the better to start fresh.

But where's the room within the metaphor
to take into account the moving front
that bundled up the rain, and memories
of balls that, rising, left the yard, or settled
into gloves in sight of multitudes?

Using an Accent

When I use an accent, it's about
the placement of the tongue, the opening
between the lips, the setting of the jaw.

Next, it's about the pace of the release
of breath, and then its force, and finally
the feeling of the carving of the air
as my tongue's tip is moving in my mouth.

And after that, remembering the feeling,
and hanging on to it, and swinging from it
like it was a rope tied to the branch
of a familiar tree, out over water
and back, but always hanging on to it.

But when I'm talking to myself, in my
own head, or praying, or not saying what
I'm thinking as I talk to someone there,
or someone far away, known or unknown
to me, or someone dead whom I will always
love, I use no accent. Or perhaps
I use the voice I first heard speak in me.

Why Don't You Get Back to Me?

At other times, in certain situations,
Silence used to indicate assent.

But when you're asking whether something's wrong,
a silence indicates the opposite.

We have more ways to reach out to each other,
but silence now may not mean anything.

Don't read it to confirm a hope or fear;
finding no place to land, the dove returned.

The bottle with its message crying out
your need for rescue, and exactly where

you can be found, is steered by certain currents.
It may never reach a destination.

You Have Reached Your Destination

At first you had to know the territory
to find your way back home. Your memory
was all you had to go on. Though details
might change, familiar features stayed the same.

Then someone made a map, whose every point
connected to a place in the terrain.
Now you could go where you had never been,
as long as you could translate from the page,

envisioning with your imagination
the real, from what was meant to represent it.
With practice, what you saw in front of you
confirmed your skill, and the mapmaker's art.

Now we take direction from a voice
which leads us point to point, while we relax
our knowledge of the territory,
loosening our sense of where we are.

How long before we lose all memory,
imagination wanes, and we are left
to drive ourselves in blind obedience
across a landscape utterly unknown?

You Want It Simple

You want it simple, but it isn't simple.
Some problems just have intricate solutions,
some will only lead to other problems.
You want it clear; you find instead it's murky.

You can have it one way or another,
but you don't know enough to make a choice.
And then it doesn't matter what you choose;
once you have your wish, it starts to change.

It doesn't really matter what you know.
When another person is in pain,
your being right is quite beside the point.
It's better that you listen and be present.

You're desperate to believe in gods and heroes
who work on your behalf, and rescue you
from evil, yet you feel you're in the right
to keep down those who only want the same.

You want someone to blame when not just one,
but all on every side deserve some blame.
And anyway it isn't yours to say;
we're all involved, and no one stands apart.

You're hoping for a villain. That's not it;
it's how the mechanism fits together,
with every one of us a moving part,
affecting and affected by each other.

You want it to be simple. Here it is.
Humble yourself before your ignorance,
don't rush to judge before you understand,
and learn to live despite uncertainty.

Your Feelings, No

The phlebotomist predicts a little pinch.
The needle disappears under your skin.
But even at her best, she sometimes fails
to find the vein. She changes up her angle
and pushes further, but no blood appears.

She mentions that this doesn't often happen,
and pokes around some more, to no avail.
Another inch of needle disappears.
Try hard not to let a grimace slip,
a wince, or sound a little yelp, or twitch.

You must keep steady as she moves the tip
and so must she. Indifferent to your pain
as she impales you – that's the way to be,
to limit it for both of you. Until
she's done, it's best to hold your feelings in.

Youth in Age

Once it's driven from the body, youth
retreats to the recesses of the mind,
where it continues to proclaim its truth.
It needn't be completely left behind.

It can live on, in a hiding place
eyes of the unbelievers never see
when noticing the wrinkles in a face,
or measuring the stiffness of a knee.

Discovering a fearlessness, it chooses
which emerging challenges to try;
granting itself permission, it refuses
to give up wonder or stop asking why.

Youth takes more practice after twenty-one.
Find someone old to show you how it's done.

ABOUT THE AUTHOR

Born in Haverhill, Mass., Al Basile was the first to receive a Master's degree from Brown University's writing program. He was the first trumpet player for Roomful of Blues in the mid-Seventies, and since the eighties has appeared as writer and horn player on albums and DVDS by Roomful founder Duke Robillard. He formed his own record company Sweetspot Records in 1998, and has released seventeen solo albums featuring almost 200 of his songs. He has been nominated eight times for a Blues Music Award, including one in 2016 as Best Contemporary Blues Album for his CD *Mid-Century Modern*.

His songs have been covered by Ruth Brown, Johnny Rawls, and the Knickerbocker All Stars. Guests on his own releases include the Blind Boys of Alabama, Sista Monica Parker, Sugar Ray Norcia, Jerry Portnoy, and jazz great Scott Hamilton.

Celebrated for his mastery of lyric writing as well as music, Al's skill with words extends to his other career as a poet: he is published regularly in leading journals and has two previous books, *A Lit House* (Winnikinni Press, 2012), and *Tonesmith* (Antrim House, 2017). He won the Meringoff Award for Poetry in 2015, and his verse radio play *Flash Blind* was featured at the HEARnow festival for American audio theater in the summer of 2020.

He was a teacher of English, music, and physics in a private Rhode Island high school for 25 years before devoting himself to music and poetry full time in 2005. He has given talks on lyric writing at Boston University, and for the last two years he has taught lyric writing, led panels, and performed at the West Chester Poetry Conference. In 2020 he became a member of the Powow River poets.

This book is set in a Garamond typeface. During the mid-fifteen hundreds, Claude Garamond — a Parisian punch-cutter — produced a refined array of book types that combined an unprecedented degree of balance and elegance, for centuries standing as the pinnacle of beauty and practicality in type-founding.

The author's reading of the poems in this book may be accessed at http://www.albasile.com/Solos_-_audio_files.html

Copies of the book are available at https://store.albasile.com/ and also at all bookstores, including Amazon.

For more concerning the work of Al Basile, visit www.antrimhousebooks.com/authors.html

www.ingramcontent.com/pod-product-compliance
Lightning Source LLC
Chambersburg PA
CBHW030322100526
44592CB00010B/529